Kristen Suzanne's
ULTIMATE Raw Vegan Chocolate Recipes

Kristen Suzanne's

ULTIMATE Raw Vegan Chocolate Recipes

Fast & Easy, Sweet & Savory Raw Chocolate
Recipes Using Raw Chocolate Powder, Raw
Cacao Nibs, and Raw Cacao Butter

by Kristen Suzanne

*Green
Butterfly
Press*

Scottsdale, Arizona

Green Butterfly Press
19550 N. Gray Hawk Drive, Suite 1042
Scottsdale, AZ 85255 USA

Library of Congress Control Number: 2009923666
Library of Congress Subject Heading:
1. Cookery (Natural foods) 2. Raw foods

ISBN: 978-0-9823722-0-3

2.0

Contents
• • • • • • • • •

**1: Raw Chocolate—
Rediscovering Chocolate's Divine Roots**   1

2: Chocolate Drinks   9

Yin Yang Smoothie 10

Inspirational Smoothie 11

Green Smoothie Au Chocolat 12

Mammer Jammer Smoothie 13

1-Minute Chocolate Nut Milk 14

Chocolate Holiday Spice Nog 15

Creamy Chocolate Vanilla Milk 16

Exotic Chocolate Milk 17

Chocolate Chlorophyll Shake 18

Mexican Hot Chocolate 19

Energizing Protein Smoothie 20

**3: Snacks, Soup,
Salad Dressing, Crackers & Breakfast**   21

Banana Chocolate Smash 22

Chocolate Powered Oatmeal 23

Warrior's Breakfast Mousse 24

Power Packed Trail Mix 25

Chocolate Hazelnut Butter Spread 26

Chocolate Chia Crackers 27

Candied Chocolate Pumpkin Seeds 28

Mesquite Spiced Chocolate Brazil Nut Crumble 30

Chocolate Cream Soup 31

Chocolate Vinaigrette 32

Chia Chocolate Pudding Snack 33

4: Desserts   35

Goddess Cream Cake 36

Chocolate Mango Tango Brownies 39

Chocolaty Nutty Buttery Treats 41

Easy Chocolate Coconut Sauce 42

Mused Chocolate Orange Vanilla Cheesecake 43

Double Chocolate Cherry Cheesecake 46

Chocolate Nutmeg Cookies 48

Raw Chocolates (Base) 49

Mint Chocolate Jazz 50

Hazelnut Hemp Chocolates 51

Caramel Chia Chocolates 52

Mayan Spiced Chocolates 53

Cinnamon Maca Chocolates 54

Lemon Orange Blossom Chocolates 55

Chocolate Bliss Chews 56

Chocolate Glaze 57

Chocolate Banana Ice Cream 58

Caramel Chocolate Sauce 59

Apricot Cacao Cookies 60

Lucy's Peanut Butter Chocolate Balls 61

Chocolate Crunch Hazelnut Macaroons 62

Brazil Nut Bark 63

Chocolate Cream Verve-a-Licious Tart 64

Chocolate Pumpkin Pie 66

Velvety Mocha Mousse 68

Pure Rush Chocolate 69

Mother Earth Chocolate 70

Fun Chocolate Banana Plant Leather 71

Raspberry Chocolate Ice Cream 72

Capri Lemon Chocolate Bars 73

Appendix A: Raw Basics 75

Nourishing Rejuvelac 98

Date Paste 100

Crème Fraiche 101

Nut/Seed Milk (regular) 102

Sweet Nut/Seed Cream (thick) 103

Raw Mustard 104

My Basic Raw Mayonnaise 105

Appendix B: Resources 107

Recipe List

• • • • • • • • • •

1-Minute Chocolate Nut Milk 14

Apricot Cacao Cookies 60

Banana Chocolate Smash 22

Brazil Nut Bark 63

Candied Chocolate Pumpkin Seeds 28

Capri Lemon Chocolate Bars 73

Caramel Chia Chocolates 52

Caramel Chocolate Sauce 59

Chia Chocolate Pudding Snack 33

Chocolate Banana Ice Cream 58

Chocolate Bliss Chews 56

Chocolate Chia Crackers 27

Chocolate Chlorophyll Shake 18

Chocolate Cream Soup 31

Chocolate Cream Verve-a-Licious Tart 64

Chocolate Crunch Hazelnut Macaroons 62

Chocolate Glaze 57

Chocolate Hazelnut Butter Spread 26

Chocolate Holiday Spice Nog 15

Chocolate Mango Tango Brownies 39

Chocolate Nutmeg Cookies 48

Chocolate Powered Oatmeal 23

Chocolate Pumpkin Pie 66

Chocolate Vinaigrette 32

Chocolaty Nutty Buttery Treats 41

Cinnamon Maca Chocolates 54

Creamy Chocolate Vanilla Milk 16

Crème Fraiche 101

Date Paste 100

Double Chocolate Cherry Cheesecake 46

Easy Chocolate Coconut Sauce 42

Energizing Protein Smoothie 20

Exotic Chocolate Milk 17

Fun Chocolate Banana Plant Leather 71

Goddess Cream Cake 36

Green Smoothie Au Chocolat 12

Hazelnut Hemp Chocolates 51

Inspirational Smoothie 11

Lemon Orange Blossom Chocolates 55

Lucy's Peanut Butter Chocolate Balls 61

Mammer Jammer Smoothie 13

Mayan Spiced Chocolates 53

Mesquite Spiced Chocolate Brazil Nut Crumble 30

Mexican Hot Chocolate 19

Mint Chocolate Jazz 50

Mother Earth Chocolate 70

Mused Chocolate Orange Vanilla Cheesecake 43

My Basic Raw Mayonnaise 105

Nourishing Rejuvelac 98

Nut/Seed Milk (regular) 102

Power Packed Trail Mix 25

Pure Rush Chocolate 69

Raspberry Chocolate Ice Cream 72

Raw Chocolates (Base) 49

Raw Mustard 104

Sweet Nut/Seed Cream (thick) 103

Velvety Mocha Mousse 68

Warrior's Breakfast Mousse 24

Yin Yang Smoothie 10

1
· · ·

Raw Chocolate—Rediscovering Chocolate's Divine Roots

> This guy found a bottle on the ocean. He opened it and out popped a genie, who gave him three wishes. The guy wished for a million dollars, and poof! There was a million dollars. Then he wished for a convertible, and poof! There was a convertible. And then, he wished he could be irresistible to all women... poof! He turned into a box of chocolates.
>
> ANONYMOUS

I wanted to write a book with recipes featuring chocolate because, quite simply... I think chocolate is wonderful. Every time I have chocolate in my mouth, I can't help but smile. For many, myself included, chocolate makes the world go 'round, and I just cannot imagine my life without it. I mean, seriously, who can deny such a decadent, versatile, extraordinarily nutritious, and enticing ingredient? Not me! *And, probably not you, if you're reading this book!*

Chocolate (otherwise referred to as cacao—pronounced "ka-kow") has been a part of my life since I was a little girl. One of my greatest childhood memories was watching *Willy Wonka & the Chocolate Factory* and dreaming of being able to eat all of that chocolate.

A BRIEF HISTORY OF CHOCOLATE

Originating in South America, chocolate has been cultivated for more than 3,000 years. In Central America and Mexico, ancient Mayans and Aztecs enjoyed chocolate in the form of a bitter, frothy drink. Although consumed by many people in society, chocolate was typically enjoyed by royalty or during sacred ceremonies. Later, when the Spanish arrived, they introduced chocolate to Europe and the love affair with chocolate began its spread across the rest of the world.

Dark chocolate has always been popular in Europe, but in 1905, Milton S. Hershey opened a factory in Hershey, Pennsylvania, to manufacture huge quantities of cheaper milk chocolate priced for the masses in America. Hershey milk chocolate bars became world-famous during World War II when they became a standard dessert in American G.I. rations. When the soldiers returned home after the war, they continued eating Hershey bars and Americans have been hooked on milk chocolate ever since.

After a half-century of cheap, mass-produced mediocrity in all food categories, Americans started yearning for something new. In the 1980's, a trend toward more gourmet foods began to gain momentum among affluent consumers, which led to a commercial renaissance in food categories like wine, coffee, and microbrewed beers, with the trend always toward fuller, richer, more sophisticated flavors for more sophisticated palates. Fast-forward to today, where I'm happy to report that dark chocolate has finally become recognized among foodies for what Europeans have known all along—namely, that its full, natural dark flavor is *freaking AMAZING* and it's a sin against nature to dilute this truly divine food with cheap fillers like milk, sugar, and wax. Yes, wax!

I'm soooo excited about this trend, not only for the good foodliness of it, but—best of all—dark chocolate is usually vegan and it's healthier, too.

THE RIGHT CHOCOLATE — RAW CHOCOLATE

I love the fact that one of my greatest pleasures in life is actually good for me. My favorite way to have chocolate is in the "raw" form—straight from the cacao bean—because raw chocolate is unrefined, unprocessed, all natural and filled with nutrients.

The health benefits of raw chocolate are significant, with a résumé that includes loads of antioxidants (and I really mean loads!) as well as magnesium, fiber, iron, calcium, zinc, copper, vitamins A, B1, B2, B3, E, and more. One of the main attractions to pure chocolate is that of the heart health benefits. The flavonoids (organic compounds) found in cacao can help prevent clogged arteries and lower blood pressure.

So, yes, raw chocolate is indeed great and offers us a number of health benefits. However, that does not mean that we should go overboard when eating it. A little bit goes a long way and moderation, as always, is important with this superfood.

RAW CHOCOLATE VERSATILITY

Raw chocolate can be used in a variety of forms—from crunchy cacao nibs, to smooth cacao powder, to creamy cacao butter—for making fabulous recipes that will knock your socks off. But that's not all. Chocolate is also versatile in that it has been used in both sweet *and savory* dishes for centuries. You'll see some wonderful examples of this versatility in the recipes that follow.

Raw Cacao Nibs

"Raw cacao nibs"—as they're commonly called—are simply cacao beans that are partially ground. They are intense in flavor (bitter because it's essentially very dark, pure chocolate) and they have a lovely crunchy texture. There are many ways to enjoy raw cacao nibs:

- Sprinkled on raw vegan ice cream, raw vegan yogurt, or even salad
- Added to trail mix
- Ground and used in crusts for cakes or pies, as well as adding them to brownies and cookies
- Blended into smoothies and nut milks

Raw Chocolate Powder

This stuff is heavenly. It's light, fluffy, delicious and can be added to many foods and recipes. Raw chocolate powder is what you're left with when you remove the oil from the cacao bean. I use raw chocolate powder in many raw vegan recipes including:

- Smoothies
- Mousse, ice cream, puddings, cake, brownies, cookies
- Soups, salad dressings, crackers, sauces
- Protein bars, nut/seed butters, and nut/seed milks

Raw Cacao Butter

The extracted oil I referred to above when making raw chocolate powder is called *cacao butter*. This is PURE DECADENCE... the smell is intoxicating. Among all the world's ingredients, raw cacao butter is truly divine.

Cacao butter can be used to take your chocolate recipes to the next level of richness and flavor. Cacao butter is also a great body and hair moisturizer, as well as an enticing massage oil.

In some of the following recipes where I use raw cacao butter, I use it in the liquid state. You can get your cacao butter into a liquid state by warming it in your dehydrator or warming it by gently using the "double-boiler" method with hot water (but you don't need it to be too hot). You do this by melting the raw cacao butter in a bowl (I use glass) that is set over a pot of hot water. If using this double-boiler method, which is quicker than the dehydrator, be sure to continuously drain off the oil as it melts every few minutes. This will prevent it from getting too hot—remember, you want to keep it raw (under 118 degrees F).

Raw Cacao Liquor

I love this product from Navitas Naturals™. Raw Cacao Liquor comes in a solid bar form, like the Raw Cacao Butter mentioned above. Where I wrote earlier that the cacao butter is the oil that is extracted (leaving the raw chocolate powder behind), this Raw Cacao Liquor is basically the oil and the powder still together. Navitas Naturals takes the whole bean and uses a cold-press process to create a rich paste (the concentrated liquor). This stuff is really cool and easy to use. When I use it in a couple of the following recipes, I melt it down using the double-boiler method or my dehydrator.

Beyond Food

Chocolate is not just for eating. More and more natural beauty care companies are using cacao butter as the primary ingredient in moisturizers, lip balms, lotions, etc. Though I've not tested it myself, many women even swear by cacao butter's ability to help prevent or help eliminate stretch marks.

Chocolate's Copy Cat—Carob

I suspect that if you're reading this book, you're probably a chocolate fan, and you don't have to replace it with carob when making recipes that call for chocolate. However, if you're making one of these recipes for a friend or loved one who is avoiding chocolate due to allergies or because you're avoiding caffeine, feel free to replace the chocolate in the following recipes with some earthy raw carob. Carob, in my opinion, is not a true replacement for the chocolate flavor, rather it lends a nice caramel note to recipes (and is still delicious).

Navitas Naturals™—Raw Vegan Chocolate Products

My kitchen is stocked with my favorite raw vegan chocolate products from Navitas Naturals, which are available at Navitas-Naturals.com as well as most Whole Foods Markets. They are a certified organic, green business that is headquartered in California. Their products are wonderfully fresh, organic, and their customer service is superb. I'm happy to recommend them to everyone.

STORING CHOCOLATE

You can keep your raw chocolate powder, raw cacao butter, raw cacao liquor, and raw cacao nibs fresh by storing them in a cool, dry place for 6–12 months. I usually store mine in the freezer or refrigerator.

SPECIAL INGREDIENTS

You'll see that I use a few unique ingredients in a couple of the recipes in this book, specifically: lucuma powder, mesquite powder, and maca powder. I get these at NavitasNaturals.com

Lucuma Powder

Lucuma is a fun ingredient that is popular in the Raw world because it's from a nutritious and sweet fruit that has a number of nutrients such as iron, fiber, niacin, calcium, and more. Navitas Naturals offers lucuma as a whole food powder, which adds a lovely sweetness to recipes with a flavor that has been described as a cross between sweet potato and maple. I love using lucuma powder in various raw recipes for smoothies, ice cream, cheesecake, nut milk, cookies, brownies, and more.

According to NavitasNaturals.com, "In coastal Peru, archaeologists have frequently found lucuma depicted on ceramics during excavations of ancient burial sites that date back thousands of years. " Pretty cool.

Mesquite Powder

Mesquite is another great ingredient to use in recipes when you're looking for a smoky, or almost malt-like, flavor. Like lucuma, mesquite powder is also popular in many raw food recipes for its flavoring properties and nutritious value. Mesquite powder contains fiber, calcium, lysine, iron, zinc, potassium, and more. I am fond of using mesquite powder in some of my recipes for smoothies, nut milk, ice cream, cookies, and more.

Maca Powder

Maca is a plant that is used as a root and medicinal herb. Many people claim it gives them tons of energy and increased stamina for exercise, long workdays, and even libido! Personally, I'm not the hugest fan of maca's flavor (to me, it smells like feet and tastes accordingly—haha), but this is one of the most popular superfoods among Raw vegans (so many people love it!), and for good reason with its reputed benefits. (Did I mention libido?)

Vanilla Bean

Vanilla is a flavor that pairs wonderfully with chocolate. You'll see vanilla bean (specifically, the seeds inside the bean) included in a couple of the recipes in this book. Vanilla beans are easy to use. Simply take your knife and slice lengthwise down the bean, only cutting through the top layer (leaving the bottom intact i.e., the surface touching the cutting board). After you slice the vanilla bean, carefully open it with your fingers. Take your knife, or a spoon, and gently scrape out the seeds.

I also have a recipe where I use the whole vanilla bean (Creamy Chocolate Vanilla Milk, see recipe, Chapter 2). In this case, simply chop up the whole vanilla bean and toss it into the blender.

PHOTOS OF RECIPES IN THIS BOOK

For enticing color photographs of the following recipes found in this book, visit KristensRaw.com/photos:

- Creamy Chocolate Vanilla Milk
- Chocolate Powered Oatmeal
- Chocolate Hazelnut Butter Spread
- Chocolate Chia Crackers
- Chocolate Cream Soup
- Goddess Cream Cake
- Mayan Spiced Chocolates
- Caramel Chocolate Sauce
- Chocolate Crunch Hazelnut Macaroons

2
• • •

Chocolate Drinks

The divine drink builds up resistance and fights fatigue. One cup of this precious drink (cocoa) lets a man walk for a whole day without food.

MONTEZUME, AZTEC EMPEROR

Drinking chocolate... mmmm I love that. These recipes are sure to fix your chocolate craving in an instant. They are decadent, delicious, easy, and fun.

Yin Yang Smoothie

Yield approximately 1 quart

I love drinking this swirling, energetic smoothie. The cool and refreshing effect from the frozen bananas (yin) opposite the spicy hot fire you feel on your tongue and the back of your throat as you swallow (yang)... well, it's enough to make anyone feel refreshingly hot.

> 1–2 cups water
>
> 3 frozen bananas, chopped
>
> 3 tablespoons organic raw chocolate powder
>
> ¾–1 red Serrano pepper (or a little habanero pepper—mega heat!)

Blend all of the ingredients until thick and creamy.

Inspirational Smoothie

Cranberries are a wonderful addition to your diet. I like to stock up on fresh cranberries when they're in season and freeze them to enjoy year round. These little red pearls of tartness present you with vitamins C & K, dietary fiber, manganese, and more. We, women, know they're wonderful for helping prevent and treat urinary tract infections (cranberries seem to work by keeping bad bacteria from sticking to your bladder).

But, that's not all. They can help lower LDL cholesterol and raise HDL ("good") cholesterol. And, get this! These ferocious warriors have five times the antioxidants of broccoli and also seem to behave as natural probiotics.

> 1 ½ cups water
>
> 3 bananas, peeled
>
> ⅓ cup fresh cranberries
>
> ½ red jalapeno or Serrano pepper, seeded
>
> 3 tablespoons fresh basil, chopped
>
> 1 ½ tablespoons raw chocolate powder

Blend all of the ingredients until smooth.

Green Smoothie Au Chocolat

Yield approximately 1–2 servings

Two of my favorite healthy ingredients… chocolate and greens! You can't go wrong with that powerful combination.

  2 cups water (more if desired)

  1 cup spinach, packed

  2 large bananas, peeled

  1 tablespoon raw chocolate powder (or more!)

  ⅛ teaspoon cinnamon

Blend all of the ingredients together and enjoy as you take in those powerful antioxidants.

Mammer Jammer Smoothie

Yield 1 serving

This is a super good smoothie. I love the combination of raw carob with dates. It gives it an almost caramel flavor. Yum!

- 1 cup water (more if desired)
- 2 bananas, peeled
- 2 soft dates, pitted
- 1 tablespoon raw cacao nibs
- 1 teaspoon raw carob powder
- pinch nutmeg

Blend all of the ingredients in a blender until smooth, adding more water to get your desired consistency.

1-Minute Chocolate Nut Milk

Yield 2 ½ cups

For those of us chocolate lovers on the run, here is a quick 1-minute nut milk you can enjoy. This can be used on cereal or raw granola, in shakes and smoothies, or just by itself. Sometimes, I even drink it for my dessert. Delish!

  2 cups water

  2–3 tablespoons raw nut or seed butter

  1 tablespoon raw agave nectar or 1–2 soft dates, pitted

  1–2 tablespoons raw chocolate powder

Blend all of the ingredients together until smooth and creamy.

Chocolate Holiday Spice Nog

Yield 1 quart

This wonderful beverage reminds me of the holidays. Enjoy this served in lovely wine goblets or glasses.

- ½ cup raw cashews
- 3 cups water (more if desired)
- ½ cup hemp seeds
- 4 soft dates, pitted
- 2 tablespoons raw chocolate powder
- 3 tablespoons raw agave nectar
- 3 cloves, crushed
- ½ teaspoon vanilla extract
- ½ teaspoon rum extract
- ½ teaspoon cinnamon
- ¼ teaspoon cardamom
- ¼ teaspoon nutmeg
- ¼ teaspoon ginger powder
- pinch Himalayan crystal salt

Place the cashews in a bowl and cover with enough water by about an inch. Let them soak for 1 hour. Drain off the water and give them a quick rinse. Blend all of the ingredients together until smooth and creamy.

Creamy Chocolate Vanilla Milk

See photo at KristensRaw.com/photos.

Yield 1 quart

Here is a terrific treat for any time of the day. I use this on cereal or raw granola, in shakes and smoothies, and sometimes I simply enjoy a tall, chilled glass of it all by itself!

- 2 ½ cups water (more if desired)
- ½ cup hemp seeds
- ½ cup raw cashews
- 1 vanilla bean, minced
- 3 tablespoons raw chocolate powder
- 3 tablespoons raw agave nectar or Date Paste (see recipe, Appendix A)
- ½ teaspoon vanilla extract

Blend all of the ingredients until smooth and creamy.

Exotic Chocolate Milk

Yield 3 cups

Ginger is a rich source of powerful antioxidants, which have anti-inflammatory properties, and there is evidence that ginger's antioxidants might help fight/inhibit the growth of certain types of cancers. Not only that, studies show ginger can also help boost the immune system.

I love this unique and sophisticated drink. In fact, this recipe is one of my mom's favorites. It's full of delicious flavors and is easy to make.

> 2 cups water
>
> 1 cup hemp seeds
>
> ¼ cup raw chocolate powder
>
> 2 tablespoons raw agave nectar or Date Paste (see recipe, Appendix A)
>
> 1 ½ teaspoons orange blossom water
>
> 1 teaspoon fresh grated ginger (or more)
>
> pinch Himalayan crystal salt (optional)

Blend all of the ingredients until smooth and creamy.

Chocolate Chlorophyll Shake

This is one awesomely nutritious shake. Wheat grass powder is an amazing source of nutrition including phytonutrients, fiber, iron, chlorophyll, folate, beta-carotene, vitamin C, protein, and more.

Kale rocks, too. It's loaded with antioxidants and phytonutrients shown to help fight cancer, aid in detoxification, and fill you up with nutrition including iron, calcium, protein, fiber, vitamins A, C, K and much more!

1 ½ cups water (or more)

2 bananas, peeled

6 strawberries, destemmed

2 leaves kale

2 tablespoons raw chocolate powder

1 tablespoon organic wheat grass powder

¼ teaspoon vanilla extract

Blend all of the ingredients together until smooth.

Mexican Hot Chocolate

Yield 2 cups

This is a deliciously warm beverage that's Raw, nourishing, and comforting. My husband and I love sipping on this in front of the fireplace during the winter months. It's wonderful.

1 ½ cups water

½ cup raw Brazil nuts

1 ½ tablespoons raw chocolate powder

1 tablespoon raw agave nectar or Date Paste (see recipe, Appendix A)

¼ teaspoon cinnamon

pinch cayenne pepper

pinch black pepper

pinch nutmeg

pinch Himalayan crystal salt

Blend all of the ingredients until smooth and warm (but not hot). This could take a couple of minutes.

Energizing Protein Smoothie

Yield approximately 1 quart

Smoothies hit the spot when I want something that is somewhat light, but that will also stay with me for a couple of hours. This smoothie is packed full with nutrients and gives me skyrocketing energy every time I drink it!

> 1 ½ cups water
>
> 2 apples, cored and chopped
>
> 1 banana, peeled
>
> 2 handfuls spinach
>
> 1 tablespoon raw chocolate powder
>
> 1 tablespoon goji berries
>
> 2 tablespoons hemp protein powder
>
> ¼ teaspoon cinnamon
>
> ⅛ teaspoon nutmeg

Blend all of the ingredients until smooth.

3
...

Snacks, Soup, Salad Dressing, Crackers & Breakfast

What use are cartridges in battle? I always carry chocolate instead.

GEORGE BERNARD SHAW

This is a unique chapter, because it is filled with both sweet and savory chocolate recipes. Most people consume chocolate in the sweet sense, but chocolate is so versatile that it is delicious as either sweet or savory.

Banana Chocolate Smash

Yield 1–2 servings

Here is a great recipe to make for breakfast. Have fun making this as you "smash" the banana with the other amazing ingredients. Oh, and by the way... it also makes a great snack at 3 am when you get home from a long night out.

 2 medium–large bananas, peeled and chopped

 1 tablespoon goji berries, dried cranberries, or dried cherries

 2 teaspoons raw chocolate powder (or more)

 2 teaspoons hemp seeds (or more)

 1 teaspoon raw cacao nibs, chopped

 1 teaspoon hemp protein powder

Place all of the ingredients in a bowl and smash it up until it's a pudding-like, chunky texture.

Chocolate Powered Oatmeal

See photo at KristensRaw.com/photos.

Yield 2 servings

A super powered breakfast... this breakfast is for true champions.

½ cup raw oats

1 banana, peeled

1 apple or pear, cored and chopped

2 tablespoons hemp seeds

1 tablespoon raw chocolate powder (or more)

1 tablespoon goji berries

2–3 teaspoons Date Paste (see recipe, Appendix A) or raw
   agave nectar

⅛ teaspoon cinnamon

pinch Himalayan crystal salt

Place the oats in a bowl and add enough water to cover the oats by about a ½ inch. Gently drape a paper towel over the bowl and allow the oats to soak like this overnight. The following morning, gently drain the oats. Process all of the ingredients in your food processor, fitted with the "S" blade.

Variations:

• For extra protein, add 1–2 tablespoons of hemp protein powder.

• For extra sweetness, add some chopped dates or raisins.

Warrior's Breakfast Mousse

Yield 2 servings (approximately 1 ¼ cups)

When I make this recipe for my husband, he eats the whole thing (so I need to make extra if I want to have any—ha ha). He loves it so much! Warrior's Breakfast Mousse is one of his most frequently requested breakfasts.

> ¼ **cup fresh squeezed orange juice**
>
> 2 **tablespoons water**
>
> 1 **avocado, pitted and peeled**
>
> 1 **banana, peeled**
>
> 4 **soft dates, pitted**
>
> 3 **tablespoons raw chocolate powder**
>
> 1 **tablespoon protein powder***
>
> ⅛ **teaspoon cinnamon**

Blend all of the ingredients until creamy. Serve immediately or chill Warrior's Breakfast Mousse in the refrigerator for up to an hour before serving.

* I really like Sun Warrior's chocolate flavored brown rice protein powder for this recipe, because it is raw, sprouted, and delicious.

Power Packed Trail Mix

I've always been a fan of trail mix because it's a quick snack to make and easy to transport. One of my favorite times for munching on this is when I'm on a long hike. It's the perfect snack while on the trail to keep me fueled with nutrients.

> **1 cup hemp seeds, raw pumpkin seeds, or raw sunflower seeds (or a mix of them all)**
> **⅓ cup currants or raisins**
> **¼ cup goji berries**
> **¼ cup raw cacao nibs**
> **pinch Himalayan crystal salt**

Place all of the ingredients in a glass mason jar and shake to mix them up.

Variations:

- The sky is the limit with the different variations for this recipe. For example, you could swap out the goji berries for dried cranberries or dried cherries. You could replace the currants with chopped dates. You could add chopped dried apricots or homemade dried blueberries. Just remember to keep the cacao nibs in it for some chocolate love.

Chocolate Hazelnut Butter Spread

See photo at KristensRaw.com/photos.

Yield 1 ¼ cups

Hazelnuts are not only great for adding a nice complementary flavor to chocolate, but they're also good for you. They contain a plant sterol that has been shown to help lower cholesterol. Hazelnuts also contain omega-3 fatty acids, as well as potassium, magnesium, fiber, vitamin E, and phosphorus.

Spread this nut butter on some Chocolate Chia Crackers (see recipe, below) and you have a real treat! Now, we're talking chocolate *on chocolate!*

   1 ½ cups raw hazelnuts

   ½ cup raw cashews

   3 tablespoons raw chocolate powder

   2–3 tablespoons coconut oil

   2 tablespoons raw agave nectar

   pinch Himalayan crystal salt

Process all of the ingredients in a food processor, fitted with the "S" blade until smooth. You may have to stop it a few times to scrape down the sides of the food processor. Store this in the refrigerator.

Chocolate Chia Crackers

See photo at KristensRaw.com/photos.

Yield 20–30 crackers or more (depends on the size cut)

1 cup chia seeds

2 cups water

Juice of 1 orange

1 apple, cored and chopped

¼ cup raw chocolate powder

2 tablespoons raw agave nectar

6 soft dates, pitted

dash Himalayan crystal salt

Soak the chia seeds for 30 minutes in a large bowl with 1 ½ cups of the water. Blend the remaining ingredients together (including the remaining ½ cup of water). Add the blended mixture to the bowl with soaked chia seeds and stir to mix. Break up any chia seed clumps with your rubber spatula or spoon. Let the mix sit, as is, for 15–30 minutes.

Spread the mixture on a dehydrator tray lined with a non-stick ParaFlexx sheet and score to desired size. (For a thinner cracker, divide between two trays.) Dehydrate at 130–140 degrees F for approximately 60 minutes. Reduce the temperature to 105 degrees F and dehydrate for another 6–8 hours. Flip the crackers onto another tray without a ParaFlexx sheet and peel off the ParaFlexx sheet already being used. Dehydrate another 6–10 hours, or until you reach your desired dryness.

Candied Chocolate Pumpkin Seeds

Yield 1 cup

I am crazy for these. They're a wonderful, super tasty, and nutritious snack. The really strange (but really cool) thing is that these actually smell and taste a little like brownies! *Weird—and addictive—but I love it!* Pumpkin seeds have a high phytosterol content, zinc, magnesium, phosphorus, potassium, fiber, protein, and more.

> 1 cup raw pumpkin seeds
>
> 2 tablespoons raw agave nectar
>
> 2 tablespoons raw chocolate powder
>
> 1 tablespoon fresh orange juice
>
> 1 teaspoon lucuma powder
>
> ½ teaspoon vanilla extract
>
> pinch Himalayan crystal salt

Place the pumpkin seeds in a bowl and cover with enough water by about an inch. Let them soak for 4–6 hours. Drain off the water and give them a quick rinse.

Stir the agave nectar, chocolate powder, orange juice, lucuma powder, vanilla, and salt together in a bowl. Add the soaked pumpkin seeds, and stir everything together until all of the pumpkin seeds are well coated.

Transfer the seeds (and any remaining sauce) onto a dehydrator tray lined with a ParaFlexx sheet. Dehydrate at 130–140 degrees

F for one hour. Lower the temperature to 105 degrees F and dehydrate another 6–9 hours. Flip the seeds onto a dehydrator tray without a ParaFlexx sheet and peel off the ParaFlexx sheet currently being used. Continue dehydrating until dry (approximately 8–14 hours).

Serving suggestions:

- These are delicious by the handful.
- Sprinkle them on your next salad.
- Top your ice cream with them.
- Take to the movies to munch on instead of popcorn.

Mesquite Spiced Chocolate Brazil Nut Crumble

Yield 1 cup

Do you need some selenium and you want to get it from a natural, whole food source? Then, look no further... eat Brazil nuts. Here is a fantastic way to enjoy them, all spiced up and fun! This crumble is delicious. You will find yourself continuously going back into the kitchen to get another handful.

> 1 cup raw Brazil nuts, chopped
>
> 1 tablespoon raw agave nectar
>
> 1 teaspoon fresh lemon juice
>
> 1 teaspoon mesquite powder
>
> 1 teaspoon chili powder
>
> ½–1 teaspoon raw chocolate powder
>
> pinch Himalayan crystal salt

Place the Brazil nuts in a bowl and cover with enough water by about an inch. Let them soak for 1 hour. Drain off the water and give them a quick rinse.

Stir the agave nectar, lemon juice, mesquite powder, chili powder, chocolate powder, and salt together in a bowl. Add the Brazil nut pieces, and stir everything together until all of the pieces of the Brazil nuts are well coated.

Transfer the nuts (and any remaining sauce) onto a dehydrator tray lined with a ParaFlexx sheet. Dehydrate at 130–140 degrees F for one hour. Lower the temperature to 105 degrees F and dehydrate until dry (approximately 12–24 hours).

Chocolate Cream Soup

See photo at KristensRaw.com/photos.

Yield 3 cups (approximately 6 servings)

This nutritious soup is for true chocolate lovers. It's not a sweet recipe; rather a deliciously unique soup best served chilled and enjoyed in a small quantity (perhaps before lunch or dinner)—a little goes a long way.

   2 cups young Thai coconut water

   ½ cup young Thai coconut meat

   ¼ cup water

   1 banana, peeled

   ½ cup raw chocolate powder

   2 tablespoons raw agave nectar

   2 strawberries, destemmed

   2 tablespoons coconut oil

   ½ teaspoon Himalayan crystal salt

   pinch cayenne pepper (or more!)

Blend all of the ingredients together until smooth.

Chocolate Vinaigrette

Yield 1 cup

What a fun and delicious way to get more chocolate into your life... with salad! My favorite way to enjoy this dressing is on top of a wonderful spinach salad with berries, oranges (peeled and segmented), and sometimes even a sprinkle of chopped cacao nibs on top. Absolutely divine!

> ½ cup raw olive oil
>
> Juice of 1 orange
>
> 2 tablespoons fresh lemon juice
>
> 2 teaspoons raw agave nectar
>
> 2 teaspoons shallot, chopped
>
> ¾ teaspoon chili powder
>
> ½ teaspoon Himalayan crystal salt (more to taste)
>
> ½ teaspoon raw chocolate powder
>
> pinch cinnamon

Blend all of the ingredients together.

Chia Chocolate Pudding Snack

Yield 1 cup

Chia seeds have been consumed for a long time (think Mayans, Aztecs, and Incans), because they are a powerhouse of nutrition. In fact, the Mayan word for strength is "chia."

⅓ cup chia seeds

1 cup water

¼ cup hemp seeds

2 tablespoons raw agave nectar

2 tablespoons raw chocolate powder

⅛ teaspoon vanilla extract

smidge Himalayan crystal salt

Place the chia seeds in a small bowl and set aside. Blend the remaining ingredients until smooth. Pour the blended hemp mixture into the bowl with the chia seeds and stir. Wait a few minutes and stir again. (You'll notice the chia seeds beginning to take on a gelatinous texture.) Wait a few minutes, again, and stir. Do the "wait and stir" once more, and then place the Chia Chocolate Pudding Snack in the refrigerator for about 15–20 minutes (or longer, if desired).

4
• • •

Desserts

The Spanish ladies of the New World are madly addicted to chocolate, to such a point that, not content to drink it several times each day, they even have it served to them in church.

JEAN-ANTHELME BRILLAT-SAVARIN
(1755–1826)

Time to really get down to chocolate business—chocolate desserts. I'm sure I don't need to say much here, but... chocolate desserts make me smile. I smile with the thought of them. I smile with each bite. I'm smiling even as I write this, thinking about one of my favorite recipes in this chapter, Goddess Cream Cake. What can I say? Chocolate makes me smile.

Goddess Cream Cake

See photo on cover and at KristensRaw.com/photos.

Yield one 8 or 9-inch springform pan

This dessert is magnificent. So magnificent, I changed the photo on the cover of this book at the last minute! Trust me, one bite and you will understand. Goddess Cream Cake is a true chocolate-lover's dessert, and with each bite I can't help but close my eyes, tip my head back, and savor it as it gently melts in my mouth. It's transcendent.

When I gave my mom a slice, here is what she had to say. "Oh my goodness! This chocolate dessert is fabulous. It makes me want to climb up on my roof, get naked, and yell at the top of my lungs that I am one lucky woman to be eating this!"

The Crust

> 1 cup raw walnuts
>
> ¼ cup raw cacao nibs
>
> ¾ cup dried coconut, shredded and unsweetened
>
> 2 teaspoons raw chocolate powder
>
> ½ cup raisins

The Filling—Base Layer

> 2 ¼ cups raw cashews
>
> ¾ cup raw agave nectar
>
> ½ cup water
>
> ½ cup raw cacao butter, liquid

2 tablespoons coconut oil

1 tablespoon almond extract

1 tablespoon coconut extract

¾ cup raw chocolate powder

⅛ teaspoon Himalayan crystal salt

2 tablespoons soy lecithin, optional

The Filling—Top Layer

1 cup raw cashews, unsoaked

½ cup water

¼ cup + 1 tablespoon raw agave nectar

¼ cup cacao butter, liquid

2 tablespoons coconut oil

1 teaspoon almond extract

1 teaspoon coconut extract

pinch Himalayan crystal salt

1 teaspoon psyllium powder

1–2 tablespoons raw cacao nibs, ground

The Crust Directions

Using a food processor, fitted with the "S" blade, grind the walnuts and cacao nibs to a coarse grind. Add the coconut and chocolate powder and pulse to mix. Add the raisins and process until the mixture begins to stick together when you press some between two of your fingers.

Press the crust mixture firmly into the bottom of your springform pan. Place in the freezer until you're ready to pour in the filling.

The Filling—Base Layer Directions

Place the cashews in a bowl and cover with enough water by about an inch. Let them soak for 1 hour. Drain off the water and give them a quick rinse.

Using a food processor, fitted with the "S" blade, process all of the ingredients, except the soy lecithin, until very smooth. This could take a few minutes and you might have to stop it a few times to scrape down the sides. Then, add the soy lecithin and process briefly to mix.

Pour the filling mixture on top of the crust and smooth the top using an offset spatula for best results. Place in the freezer for 1–2 hours to set.

The Filling—Top Layer Directions

Grind the cashews into a powder using your blender. Add the remaining ingredients, except the psyllium powder and ground cacao nibs, and blend until creamy. Add the psyllium powder and blend briefly to mix. Pour into a small bowl and set aside until you're ready to spread it on top of the filling base. After the filling base has set in the freezer, pour the filling top layer on top, and smooth with an offset spatula.

Sprinkle the ground cacao nibs on top. Place in the freezer for an hour or so, and then you can transfer to the refrigerator until you're ready to eat. Goddess Cream Cake will stay fresh in the refrigerator for up to a week, or in your freezer for 6–12 months, when stored in an airtight container.

Chocolate Mango Tango Brownies

Yield one 8 × 8 glass baking dish

These are unique, fun, and scrumptious. They have a wonderfully earthy flavor, compliments of the Brazil nuts and *Buckies*.

1 cup raw Brazil nuts

2 tablespoons raw cacao nibs

¼ cup raw chocolate powder

1 cup *Buckies**

¾ cup dried mango, cut or torn into small pieces, packed

5 soft dates, pitted

3 tablespoons raw agave nectar

1 tablespoon coconut oil

pinch Himalayan crystal salt

Using a food processor, fitted with the "S" blade, grind the Brazil nuts and cacao nibs into a coarse grind. Add the chocolate powder and Buckies and process to mix and break up the Buckies. Add the remaining ingredients and process until the mixture begins to stick together when gently pressed between two of your fingers. Press the mixture into a glass baking dish and chill for an hour or so.

Serving suggestion:

- My favorite way to enjoy these is topped with raw vegan ice cream.

* To make Buckies, soak raw buckwheat overnight (make a lot, like 4 cups or more, so you have plenty on hand—I also love adding these to salads, raw granola cereals, on top of raw ice cream or yogurt, and more). Drain them the next morning and give them a quick rinse. Place them in a colander over a bowl. You can gently lay a paper towel over the colander. Allow them to sprout for two days, rinsing and draining 1–2 times daily.

Dehydrate your sprouted Buckies at 105 degrees F until dry (usually 6–10 hours). Leftover Buckies will keep for at least six months when stored in an airtight container (glass mason jar is perfect) in your refrigerator.

Chocolaty Nutty Buttery Treats

Yield approximately 21 treats

Watch out! Warning! Beware! These are amazing and you might find yourself eating a few at a time. (Don't say I didn't warn you!) Although these aren't entirely Raw (because they contain peanut butter), they're still fabulous, vegan, heavenly, and deliciously rich. Enjoy one with a nice warm cup of Teeccino™ or organic herbal tea.

⅔ cup raw cacao butter, liquid

½ cup raw almond butter

½ cup peanut butter*

¼ cup raw agave nectar

¼ cup raw chocolate powder

1 teaspoon vanilla extract

¼ teaspoon cinnamon

dash Himalayan crystal salt

Process all of the ingredients in a food processor, fitted with the "S" blade, until mixed well. Transfer the mixture to a bowl and place in the refrigerator for about 15 minutes to firm up. Use a tablespoon measurement to spoon out the batter (I like using a tablespoon size ice cream scoop). Place back in the refrigerator for another 15 minutes to solidify completely.

* I only use all natural, organic peanut butter (*plain,* as in the only ingredient in it is peanuts).

Easy Chocolate Coconut Sauce

Yield 1 ¾ cups

Here is a great recipe for a wonderful sauce that is perfect drizzled over fresh fruit or vegetables, raw ice cream (or cheesecake or brownie), as a delicious addition to your smoothie, or just by the spoonful.

1 cup raw agave nectar

½ cup coconut oil

⅓ cup raw chocolate powder

1 ¾ teaspoons coconut extract

Blend all of the ingredients together.

Mused Chocolate Orange Vanilla Cheesecake

Yield one 8 or 9-inch springform pan

My muse for this recipe happened while driving one night and listening to the song, *Hey Pretty,* by the artist Poe. I had my car's sunroof and windows open with the balmy Arizona night weather blowing through my hair. I pulled the car over, grabbed a scrap of paper and a pen, and scribbled down a list of ingredients.

The Crust

> 1 ½ cups raw pecans
>
> ½ cup hemp seeds
>
> pinch Himalayan crystal salt
>
> 2 teaspoons raw chocolate powder
>
> 1 teaspoon lucuma powder
>
> ½ vanilla bean, scraped*
>
> 1 teaspoon freshly grated orange zest
>
> 9 soft dates, pitted and chopped

The Filling

> 3 cups cashews
>
> ¾ cup raw agave nectar
>
> ½ cup fresh lemon juice
>
> 3 tablespoons water
>
> 1 tablespoon orange zest, freshly grated

1 tablespoon orange extract

2 tablespoons lucuma powder

1 vanilla bean, scraped*

1 cup coconut oil

¾ cup + 1 tablespoon raw chocolate powder

2 tablespoons soy lecithin

The Orange Vanilla Coulis

3 oranges, peeled, seeded, and chopped

½ vanilla bean, scraped*

5 soft dates, pitted

¼ teaspoon orange extract

The Crust Directions

Process the pecans in a food processor, fitted with the "S" blade, until coarsely ground. Add the hemp seeds and salt, and process to thoroughly incorporate. Add the chocolate powder, lucuma powder, vanilla bean, and orange zest, and process briefly to mix. Add the dates and process until the mixture begins to stick together when gently pressed between two of your fingers.

Press the crust mixture firmly into the bottom of an 8 or 9-inch round springform pan. Place in the freezer while you make the filling.

The Filling Directions

Place the cashews in a bowl and cover with enough water by about an inch. Let them soak for 1 hour. Drain off the water and give them a quick rinse.

Blend all of the ingredients, except the soy lecithin, in a food processor until creamy (5–7 minutes). You may need to stop every couple of minutes to scrape down the sides.

Add the soy lecithin and briefly process to mix. Pour the filling on top of the crust and smooth the top of it with an offset spatula.

Place the cheesecake in your refrigerator for a couple of hours to set (or you can use your freezer). Mused Chocolate Orange Vanilla Cheesecake will stay fresh for up to a week, when stored in an airtight container, in your refrigerator. Or, freeze it for 6–12 months.

The Coulis Directions

Blend all of the ingredients together until smooth. Serve 1–2 tablespoons of coulis with each slice of cheesecake.

---

* To get the contents out of a vanilla bean: carefully slice it open, lengthwise, through the top layer of the bean. Using your knife, or a spoon, gently scrape out the seeds.

Double Chocolate Cherry Cheesecake

Yield one 8 or 9-inch springform pan

My brother's favorite candy is chocolate covered cherries. I decided to make him a similar dessert that is delicious and healthier.

The Crust

1 ¾ cups raw pecans or walnuts

½ cup raw cacao nibs

⅛ teaspoon Himalayan crystal salt

¾ teaspoon cherry extract

1 tablespoon raw chocolate powder

¾ cup raisins

The Filling

3 cups raw cashews

½ cup raw agave nectar

6 soft dates, pitted

½ cup fresh lemon juice

¼ cup water

2 teaspoons cherry extract

1 cup coconut oil

¾ cup raw chocolate powder

2 tablespoons soy lecithin

The Coulis

1 (10oz) bag frozen cherries, thawed

¼ cup raw agave nectar

1 teaspoon fresh lemon juice

pinch cinnamon

The Crust Directions

Grind the nuts, cacao nibs and salt in a food processor, fitted with the "S" blade, until coarsely ground. Add the cherry extract and chocolate powder and pulse to thoroughly combine. Add the raisins and process until the mixture sticks together when gently pressed between your fingers. Press the crust mixture firmly into the bottom of the springform pan. Place in the freezer while you make the filling.

The Filling Directions

Place the cashews in a bowl and cover with enough water by about an inch. Let them soak for 1 hour. Drain off the water and give them a quick rinse.

Blend all of the ingredients, except the soy lecithin in a food processor until creamy (5–7 minutes). You may need to stop every couple of minutes to scrape down the sides. Add the soy lecithin and briefly process to mix. Pour the filling on top of the crust and smooth the top of it with an offset spatula.

Place the cheesecake in your refrigerator for a couple of hours to set (or you can use your freezer).

The Coulis Directions

Blend all of the ingredients together and serve a tablespoon (or more) over each slice of cheesecake.

Chocolate Nutmeg Cookies

Yield 10–15 cookies, depending on the size you prefer

One of the reasons I love these cookies is because no equipment is required to make them. They're easy and will take you only a few minutes to make. Everyone I know who has tried these cookies has fallen in love with them.

½ cup raw almond butter

½ cup dried coconut, shredded and unsweetened

½ cup raisins

2 tablespoons raw agave nectar

1 tablespoon raw chocolate powder

1 ½ teaspoons raw cacao nibs

¼ teaspoon vanilla extract

dash cinnamon

pinch Himalayan crystal salt

1–2 pinches nutmeg

Stir everything together in a bowl with a spoon (large bowl and spoon if you're making a double or triple batch). Then, take a moment and mash it together with your hands. Yes, it's sticky and gooey, but it's fun and you still have to roll them so you'll be getting sticky and gooey anyway. Using a 1-tablespoon measured amount of cookie batter, roll them into balls.

Raw Chocolates (Base)

Yield ½ cup base (approximately 12–13 chocolates)

Do you want simple, pure, basic, but also delicious, nutritious, and easy raw vegan, bite-sized chocolates? Well, here you go. Once your cacao butter is in liquid form, this recipe takes only minutes to prepare and it's so dang good! I always have these in a *ready-to-toss-in-the-air-and-catch-in-my-mouth* stash in the refrigerator.

> ¼ cup + 2 tablespoons raw cacao butter, liquid
>
> 2 tablespoons raw agave nectar
>
> ⅓ cup raw chocolate powder
>
> 1 ½ tablespoons lucuma powder

Stir all of the ingredients together well. This "base" recipe is delicious as is, and ready to be poured into candy molds or mini candy paper cups. Place in the freezer to set for about 10 minutes. I usually use candy molds that hold about 2 teaspoons per mold, making the perfect sized chocolates to enjoy.

For more fun with Raw Chocolates, use the following flavoring recipes!

Mint Chocolate Jazz

Mmmm… Two of my favorite flavors: chocolate and mint. I can't get enough of these delicious raw vegan chocolates.

½ cup Raw Chocolates (Base)

¼ teaspoon mint extract

Stir the ingredients together and pour into candy molds or mini candy paper cups, and place in the freezer to set for about 10 minutes.

Hazelnut Hemp Chocolates

Hazelnut is a strong and decadent flavor, making these a delicious gourmet treat.

> ½ cup Raw Chocolates (Base)
> ½ teaspoon hazelnut extract
> 3–4 tablespoons hemp seeds

Stir the Raw Chocolates (Base) and hazelnut extract together and pour into candy molds or mini candy paper cups, leaving room for the hemp seeds. Sprinkle the hemp seeds on top of each chocolate. Place in the freezer to set for about 10 minutes.

Caramel Chia Chocolates

Caramel and chocolate always taste great together. The chia seeds add a fun texture to these raw vegan goodies.

> ½ cup Raw Chocolates (Base)
> 1 tablespoon chia seeds
> dash caramel extract

Stir the ingredients together and pour into candy molds or mini candy paper cups, and place in the freezer to set for about 10 minutes. (The chia seeds give these such a lovely and fun texture... kind of like a Nestle Crunch™).

For more caramel love, dip these Caramel Chia Chocolates into Caramel Chocolate Sauce (see recipe, Chapter 4).

Mayan Spiced Chocolates

See photo at KristensRaw.com/photos.

½ cup Raw Chocolates (Base)

⅛ teaspoon cinnamon extract

⅛ teaspoon vanilla extract

⅛ teaspoon chili powder

pinch cayenne pepper

Stir the ingredients together and pour into candy molds or mini candy paper cups, and place in the freezer to set for about 10 minutes.

Cinnamon Maca Chocolates

Many people love pairing maca and raw chocolate together for a real boost in energy.

    ½ cup Raw Chocolates (Base)

    ½ teaspoon maca powder (or more)

    ⅛ teaspoon cinnamon

    dash allspice

Stir the ingredients together and pour into candy molds or mini candy paper cups, and place in the freezer to set for about 10 minutes.

Lemon Orange Blossom Chocolates

Floral, unique, and very gourmet. That's what I think each time I have these.

- ½ **cup Raw Chocolates (Base)**
- ½ **teaspoon fresh lemon zest**
- ¼ **teaspoon lemon extract**
- ¼ **teaspoon orange blossom water (or more)**

Stir the ingredients together and pour into candy molds or mini candy paper cups, and place in the freezer to set for about 10 minutes.

Chocolate Bliss Chews

Yield ¾ cup

These are fun, easy, and so wonderfully delicious. The last time I made these for a gathering of family and friends everyone unanimously agreed—you'll experience total bliss after having one of these.

⅓ cup raw agave nectar

¼ cup Artisana's Amazon Bliss*

¼ cup raw chocolate powder

2 tablespoons coconut oil

2 tablespoons coconut butter

¼ teaspoon vanilla extract

¼ teaspoon ginger powder

⅛ teaspoon cinnamon

Blend all of the ingredients together and pour into candy paper cups or molds. Refrigerate or freeze until ready to enjoy.

* Available in most Whole Foods Markets or online.

Chocolate Glaze

Yield approximately 1 cup

Use this fabulous recipe on fresh fruit or add a tablespoon of it to your nut milk or smoothie. It's also perfect on top of Raw ice cream! And, of course, it's simply delicious on a spoon all by itself.

> **1 young Thai coconut (meat and water)**
>
> **¼ cup raw agave nectar or Date Paste (see recipe, Appendix A)**
>
> **⅓ cup raw chocolate powder**

Blend all of the ingredients in a blender until smooth.

Chocolate Banana Ice Cream

Yield 2 cups

My family loves when I make this recipe and top it with Caramel Chocolate Sauce (see recipe, next page).

1 ½ cups raw cashews

1 banana, peeled

½ cup raw agave nectar

1 tablespoon water

2 tablespoons coconut oil

⅓ cup raw chocolate powder

⅛ teaspoon vanilla extract

Place the cashews in a bowl and cover with enough water by about an inch. Let them soak for 1 hour. Drain off the water and give them a quick rinse.

Blend all of the ingredients together until creamy. Pour the ice cream mixture into a shallow dish (8 × 8 glass baking dish works great), cover and freeze. Alternatively, you can use an ice cream maker and follow the manufacturer's instructions.

Variation:

- Before freezing, stir in cacao nibs or chopped raw nuts.

Caramel Chocolate Sauce

See photo at KristensRaw.com/photos.

Yield 1 cup

Look out! This is so delicious; you'll think you're in heaven when you taste it! I love having this sauce on raw vegan ice cream, over fruit, or simply by the spoonful! What a wonderful treat to always have in your refrigerator.

¼ cup water

¼ cup + 2 tablespoons raw agave nectar

7 dates, pitted, soaked 30 minutes, and drained

3 tablespoons coconut oil

1 tablespoon raw carob powder

2 tablespoons raw chocolate powder

pinch Himalayan crystal salt

dash caramel extract

Blend all of the ingredients together until smooth.

Apricot Cacao Cookies

Yield 20–30 cookies

This is a fun and tasty cookie recipe that uses a variety of neat ingredients.

¼ cup + 2 tablespoons raw pecans

3 tablespoons raw cacao nibs

¼ cup dried coconut, shredded and unsweetened

¼ teaspoon almond extract

pinch cayenne pepper

pinch Himalayan crystal salt

¼ cup hemp seeds

5 soft dates, pitted and chopped

½ cup dried apricots, diced

Using a food processor, fitted with the "S" blade, grind the pecans and cacao nibs to a coarse grind. Add the coconut, almond extract, cayenne and salt, and process to mix.

Add the remaining ingredients and process until the mixture holds together when pressed between two of your fingers. Using a tablespoon, scoop the batter out and gently roll into balls. Flatten into cookies.

Lucy's Peanut Butter Chocolate Balls

Yield 18–20 balls

One of my favorite TV shows to watch with my mom is *I Love Lucy*. We giggle non-stop. If I were pressed to pick a favorite episode, it would be the famous one... you can probably guess... the one where Lucy and Ethel sort chocolates on a conveyor belt in a candy factory. I'm laughing right now thinking about it. In honor of the *Candy Factory* episode, here are Lucy's Peanut Butter Chocolate Balls.

Although these aren't entirely Raw (because of the peanut butter), they are so delicious and fun.

> ¾ cup peanut butter*
>
> ¼ cup raw agave nectar
>
> ¼ cup dried coconut, shredded and unsweetened
>
> ¼ cup coconut oil
>
> ¼ cup + 1 tablespoon raw chocolate powder
>
> dash Himalayan crystal salt

Process all of the ingredients in a food processor, fitted with the "S" blade until mixed. Transfer the mixture to a bowl and place in the refrigerator for about 15 minutes to firm up. Use a tablespoon measurement to spoon out the batter (I like using a tablespoon size ice cream scoop). Place back in the refrigerator for another 15 minutes to solidify completely.

---

* I use all natural, organic peanut butter (*plain*, the only ingredient in it is peanuts).

Chocolate Crunch Hazelnut Macaroons

See photo at KristensRaw.com/photos.

Yield 35 macaroons

1 cup raw hazelnuts

1 cup raw chocolate powder

1 cup dried coconut, shredded and unsweetened

1 cup raw agave nectar

⅔ cup coconut butter*

½ cup raw cacao nibs

¾ teaspoon cinnamon

¼ teaspoon Himalayan crystal salt

Using a food processor, fitted with the "S" blade, grind the hazelnuts to a fairly medium/fine grind. Transfer to a large bowl and add the remaining ingredients. Stir all the ingredients together well by hand, or use a mixer with a paddle attachment to make it easier. Use a tablespoon measurement to spoon out the batter and place on a cookie sheet (I like using a tablespoon size ice cream scoop). Freeze for approximately an hour and enjoy.

Serving suggestion:

- I enjoy these straight from the freezer or refrigerator. When I take them to a party, I put them in the host's refrigerator, or freezer, until I'm ready to serve them. If they sit at room temperature they get a little soft.

* See Resources, Appendix B

Brazil Nut Bark

Yield approximately 2 cups

½ cup raw Brazil nuts

½ cup cacao butter, liquid

½ cup raw chocolate powder

2 tablespoons raw agave nectar

Slice the Brazil nuts and set aside in a small bowl. Stir the remaining ingredients together in a separate bowl until smooth. Pour the chocolate mixture over the Brazil nuts and stir so that the nuts are thoroughly coated with the chocolate.

Pour the mixture onto a plate or tray lined with wax paper. Place in the freezer for 10–15 minutes. Break it apart and enjoy! Brazil Nut Bark will stay fresh for 6–12 months, when stored in an airtight container in the freezer.

Variations:

- After pouring the mixture onto the plate, sprinkle some chopped dried cherries or raisins on top.
- Another great option is sprinkling chia seeds on top of the bark for a real fun texture. It kind of reminds me of Nestle Crunch™.

Chocolate Cream Verve-a-Licious Tart

Yield one 9-inch tart

The Crust

⅓ cup raw cacao nibs

1 ¼ cups dried coconut, shredded and unsweetened

1 cup hemp seeds

¼ teaspoon Himalayan crystal salt

dash cayenne pepper

¼ cup raw agave nectar

5 soft dates, pitted

The Filling

5 dates, pitted, soaked 30 minutes, drained

¾ cup young Thai coconut water

meat from one young Thai coconut (at least ½ cup)

½ cup raw agave nectar

1 avocado, pitted and peeled

1 tablespoon green powder* (or more)

1 tablespoon hemp protein powder (or more)

¾ cup raw chocolate powder

1 teaspoon maca powder (optional)

½ teaspoon vanilla extract

The Sweet Strawberry Coulis

1 (10oz) bag frozen strawberries, thawed (or fresh, destemmed)

¼ cup raw agave nectar

The Crust Directions

Grind the cacao nibs in your food processor, fitted with the "S" blade, until they are broken up nicely into somewhat of a coarse powder. Add the coconut, hemp seeds, salt and cayenne, and process for a few seconds as you incorporate all of the ingredients together. Add the agave nectar and dates, and process until the mixture starts to stick together briefly when pressed together between your fingers.

Press the crust into the tart pan until it's smoothly and firmly inside the pan. This crust is a little sticky, so using some coconut oil on your hands, or a tool used to press it in (spatula, for example), can help. Place the crust in the freezer while you make the filling.

The Filling Directions

Blend all of the ingredients until creamy. Pour the filling on top of the crust. Place the pie in the freezer for 1–2 hours to set.

The Coulis Directions

Blend the ingredients together. Drizzle some coulis on each slice of tart served.

---

* My favorite brand is Vitamineral Green (visit KristensRaw.com/store for details), but new green powders are always being introduced and I experiment with many of them.

Chocolate Pumpkin Pie

Yield one 8-inch springform pan

This was one of those recipes that came to me just as I was falling asleep (this happens quite often, so I keep a pen and paper on my nightstand). My poor husband—*ha ha*—so often we're drifting off to sleep and I roll over, turn on the light, and start scribbling down recipe ideas. I promise you though, he doesn't complain... especially since he gets to eat all of my crazy, middle-of-the-night recipes.

Note: It's easier to make the filling part of this recipe using a high-powered blender. If you don't have one you might consider using a food processor, fitted with the "S" blade.

The Crust

  1 ¼ cups raw pecans

  ½ cup raw cacao nibs

  ½ cup raisins

  2 teaspoons raw agave nectar

  pinch Himalayan crystal salt

The Filling

  1 ½ cups raw cashews

  1 ¼ cups water

  ½ cup + 2 tablespoons raw cacao butter, liquid

  1 cup Date Paste (see recipe, Appendix A)

½ cup raw chocolate powder

2 cups carrots, chopped (room temperature)

2 ⅓ tablespoons pumpkin pie spice

2 tablespoons raw agave nectar

1 teaspoon mesquite powder

1 teaspoon vanilla extract

¼ teaspoon maple extract

dash Himalayan crystal salt

1 ⅓ tablespoons soy lecithin

The Crust Directions

Grind the pecans and cacao nibs in your food processor, fitted with the "S" blade, into a coarse texture. Add the raisins, agave nectar, and salt and process until the mixture begins to stick together when gently pressed between two of your fingers. Press the crust mixture firmly into the bottom of a springform pan and place in the freezer while you make the filling.

The Filling Directions

Place the cashews in a bowl and cover with enough water by about an inch. Let them soak for 1 hour. Drain off the water and give them a quick rinse.

Blend all of the ingredients, except the soy lecithin, until creamy. Add the soy lecithin and pulse briefly to incorporate. Pour the filling on top of the crust. Smooth the top with an offset spatula. Place the pie in the freezer for 1–2 hours to set. Stored in an airtight container in the refrigerator, Chocolate Pumpkin Pie will stay fresh for 5–7 days (or 6–12 months in the freezer).

Velvety Mocha Mousse

Yield approximately 1 ¼ cups

If you like the flavors of coffee and chocolate, then you'll adore this creamy and delicious mousse. The smooth, whipped texture along with the taste experience is something you don't want to miss.

3 tablespoons water

1 avocado, pitted and peeled

¼ cup + 2 tablespoons raw agave nectar

¼ cup + 2 tablespoons raw chocolate powder

1 tablespoon coconut butter

1 teaspoon coffee extract

Blend all of the ingredients until smooth and creamy.

Serving suggestion:

• Let this chill in the refrigerator for approximately one hour before serving.

Pure Rush Chocolate

Yield 4 servings

Here is another simple, quick, and awesome raw vegan chocolate recipe that totally hits my chocolate button every time.

   ¼ cup + 2 tablespoons raw cacao liquor, liquid

   1 ½ tablespoons raw agave nectar

   1 tablespoon lucuma powder

   2 teaspoons raw cacao nibs, chopped

   ½ teaspoon vanilla extract

   ⅛ teaspoon cayenne pepper

Stir the ingredients together in a small bowl until smooth. Spread the chocolate mixture onto a plate lined with wax paper. Freeze for 10–15 minutes. Break into pieces.

Mother Earth Chocolate

Yield 6–8 servings

This recipe is filled with goodness, just like Mother Earth. You'll see all kinds of neat nutritious ingredients in this fun chocolate recipe.

½ cup + 2 tablespoons raw cacao liquor, liquid

2 tablespoons raw agave nectar

1 tablespoon chia seeds

1 ½ teaspoons green powder

¼ teaspoon vanilla extract

dash cinnamon

dash dulse granules or flakes

Stir the ingredients together in a small bowl until smooth. For an old-fashioned, rustic look, spread the chocolate mixture onto a plate lined with wax paper, freeze for 10–15 minutes, and break the chocolate into pieces. Alternatively, you can spoon them into individual dollop-sized servings before freezing.

Fun Chocolate Banana Plant Leather

Yield 1–2 servings

3 tablespoons water

2 bananas, peeled

2 tablespoons raw chocolate powder

Blend the ingredients until smooth. Pour the mixture onto a dehydrator tray lined with a ParaFlexx sheet and dehydrate at 130–140 degrees F for one hour. Turn the temperature down to 105 degrees F and continue dehydrating another 5–7 hours. Flip the plant leather onto another dehydrator tray (no ParaFlexx needed) and peel off the current ParaFlexx sheet being used. Dehydrate another 5–10 hours, or until dry.

Variations:

- Stir in chopped cacao nibs and/or dried coconut. Add the seeds of a vanilla bean, or add an extract flavoring such as vanilla, almond, maple, cherry, or hazelnut.

Serving suggestions:

- Enjoy plain, as is.
- Use as a dessert pizza crust and spread raw nut butter on it, topped with fresh berries.
- Eat as a crepe, filled with raw chocolate mousse, dried coconut, and topped with sweet berry coulis (use toothpicks to hold together).

Raspberry Chocolate Ice Cream

Yield approximately 2 cups

⅔ cup raw cashews

⅓ cup raw agave nectar

1 (10 oz) bag frozen raspberries (thawed)

¼ cup raw chocolate powder

2 tablespoons raw cacao butter, liquid

2 teaspoons vanilla extract

Grind the cashews into a fine grind using your blender. Add the remaining ingredients and blend until very smooth. You can add a little water to help if needed. If any of the raw cacao butter hardens on the sides of the blender, because the raspberries are cold, simply scrape if off the blender sides and continue blending until smooth. Alternatively, you can wait until your thawed raspberries are closer to room temperature before blending.

Pour the mixture into a small, shallow glass baking dish and freeze overnight. Or, you can use an ice cream maker and follow the manufacturer's instructions.

Variations:

- For some added texture, chocolate, and crunch, stir in 1–2 tablespoons of chopped raw cacao nibs.
- Sprinkle chopped raw almonds or pecans on top just before serving, for a wonderful spin on the recipe.
- Use strawberries or blueberries in place of the raspberries.

Capri Lemon Chocolate Bars

Yield one 8-inch glass baking dish

These bars are dense and full of flavor. Sometimes I have one for dessert and sometimes I eat a little one for breakfast with a cup of organic herbal tea.

The Bars

2 cups raw macadamia nuts

2 ½ teaspoons lemon extract

3 tablespoons raw agave nectar

¼ cup fresh lemon juice

10 dates, pitted, soaked 30 minutes and drained

½ cup dried apple, soaked 30 minutes and drained

The Frosting

8 dates, pitted, soaked 30 minutes (reserve "soak water")

2 tablespoons fresh lemon juice

3–4 tablespoons "soak water" from the dates

3 tablespoons raw chocolate powder

2 tablespoons raw agave nectar

2 tablespoons chopped macadamia nuts

¼ cup coconut oil

The Bars Directions

Process the nuts in a food processor, fitted with the "S" blade, until coarsely ground. Add the lemon extract, agave nectar, and lemon juice, and process to mix. Add the dates and dried apple and process until the mixture is thoroughly incorporated. Press (or spread) the mixture into the bottom of the glass baking dish. Place in the refrigerator or freezer while you make the frosting.

The Frosting Directions

Blend all of the ingredients together (don't worry about blending the macadamia nuts until entirely smooth if you don't want; they can add a nice texture to the frosting). Spread on top of the bars.

Appendix A
• • • • • • • • • •

Raw Basics

This "Raw Basics" appendix is a brief introduction to Raw for those who are new to the subject. It is the same in all of my recipe books.

WHY RAW?

Living the Raw vegan lifestyle has made me a more effective person... in everything I do. I get to experience pure, sustainable all-day-long energy. My body is in perfect shape and I gain strength and endurance in my exercise routine with each passing day. My relationships are the best they've ever been, because I'm happy and I love myself and my life. My headaches have ceased to exist, and my skin glows with the radiance of brand new life, which is exactly how I feel. Raw vegan is the best thing that has ever happened to me.

Whatever your passion is in life (family, business, exercise, meditation, hobbies, etc.), eating Raw vegan will take it to unbelievable new heights. Raw vegan food offers you the most amazing benefits—physically, mentally, and spiritually. It is *the* ideal choice for your food consumption if you want to become the healthiest and best "you" possible. Raw vegan food is for people who want to live longer while feeling younger. It's for people who want to feel vibrant and alive, and want to enjoy life like never before. All I ever have to say to someone is, "Just try it for yourself." It will change your life. From simple to gourmet, there's always something for everyone, and it's delicious. Come into the world of Raw with me, and experience for yourself the most amazing health *ever*.

Are you ready for your new lease on life? The time is now. Let's get started!

SOME GREAT THINGS TO KNOW BEFORE DIVING INTO THESE RECIPES

Organic Food

According to the Organic Trade Association, "Organic agricultural production benefits the environment by using earth-friendly agricultural methods and practices." Here are some facts that show why organic farming is "the way to grow."

Choosing organically grown foods is one of the most important choices we can make. According to Environmental Working Group, "The growing consensus among scientists is that small doses of some pesticides and other chemicals can cause lasting damage to human health, especially during fetal development and early childhood."

I use organic produce and products for pretty much everything when it comes to my food. There are very few exceptions, and that would be if the recipe called for something I just can't get organic such as jicama, certain seasonings, or any random ingredient that my local health food store is not able to procure from an organic grower for whatever reason.

If you think organic foods are too expensive, then start in baby steps and buy a few things at a time. Realize that you're probably going to spend less money in the long run on health problems as your health improves, and going organic is one way to facilitate that.

The more people who choose organic, the lower the prices will be in the long run. Until then, if people complain about the prices of organic produce, all I can say is, "Your health is worth it!" Personally, I'm willing to spend more on it and sacrifice other things in my life if necessary. I don't need the coolest car on the block, I want the healthiest food going into my body. I like what Alice Waters says, "Why wouldn't you want to spend most of your money on food? Food is nourishment and good health. It is the most important thing in life, really."

Vote with your dollar! Here is something I do to help further this cause and you can, too. When I eat at a restaurant I always write on the bill, "I would eat here more if you served organic food." Can you imagine what would happen if we all did this?

Bottom Line: It is essential to use organic ingredients for many reasons:

1. The health benefits — superior nutrition, reduced intake of chemicals and heavy metals and decreased exposure to carcinogens. Organic food has been shown to have up to 300% more nutrition than conventionally grown, non-organic produce. And, a very important note for pregnant women: pesticides could cross the placenta and get to the growing life inside of you. Make organics an extra priority if you are pregnant.

2. To have the very best tasting food ever — use organic ingredients! I've had people tell me in my raw food demonstration classes that they never knew vegetables tasted so good — and one of the main reasons is because I only use organic.

3. Greater variety of heirloom fruits and vegetables is the result of growing organic produce.

4. Cleaner rivers and waterways for our earth and its inhabitants, along with minimized topsoil erosion. Overall, organic farming builds up the soil better, reduces carbon dioxide from the air, and has many environmental benefits.

Going Organic on a Budget

Going organic on a budget is not impossible. Here are things to keep in mind that will help you afford it:

1. Buy in bulk. Ask the store you frequent if they'll give you a deal for buying certain foods by the case. (Just make sure it's a case of something that you can go through in a timely fashion so it doesn't go to waste). Consider this for bananas or greens especially if you drink lots of smoothies or green juice, like I do.

2. See if local neighbors, family or friends will share the price of getting cases of certain foods. When you do this, you can go beyond your local grocery store and contact great places (which deliver nationally) such as Boxed Greens (BoxedGreens.com) or Diamond Organics (Diamond Organics.com). Maybe they'll extend a discount if your order goes above a certain amount or if you get certain foods by the case. It never hurts to ask.

3. Pay attention to organic foods that are not very expensive to buy relative to the conventional prices (bananas, for example). Load up on those.

4. Be smart when picking what you buy as organic. Some

conventionally grown foods have higher levels of pesticides than others. For those, go organic. Then, for foods that are not sprayed as much, you can go conventional. Avocados, for example, aren't sprayed too heavily so you could buy those as conventional. Here is a resource that keeps an updated list: foodnews.org/walletguide.php

5. Buy produce that is on sale. Pay attention to which organic foods are on sale for the week and plan your menu around that. Every little bit adds up!

6. Grow your own sprouts. Load up on these for salads, soups, and smoothies. Very inexpensive. Buy the organic seeds in the bulk bins at your health food store or buy online and grow them yourself. Fun!

7. Buy organic seeds/nuts in bulk online and freeze. Nuts and seeds typically get less expensive when you order in bulk from somewhere like Sun Organic (SunOrganic.com). Take advantage of this and freeze them (they'll last the year!). Do the same with dried fruits/dates/etc. And remember, when you make a recipe that calls for expensive nuts, you can often easily replace them with a less expensive seed such as sunflower or pumpkin seeds.

8. Buy seasonally; hence, don't buy a bunch of organic berries out of season (i.e., eat more apples and bananas in the fall and winter). Also, consider buying frozen organic fruits, especially when they're on sale!

9. Be content with minimal variety from time to time. Organic spinach banana smoothies are inexpensive. You can change it up for fun by adding cinnamon one day, nutmeg another, vanilla extract yet another. Another inexpensive meal or snack is a spinach apple smoothie. Throw in

a date or some raisins for extra pizazz. It helps the budget when you make salads, smoothies, and soups with ingredients that tend to be less expensive such as carrots (year round), bananas (year round), zucchini and cucumbers (in the summer), etc.

Kristen Suzanne's Tip: A Note About Herbs

Hands down, fresh herbs taste the best and have the highest nutritional value. While I recommend fresh herbs whenever possible, you can substitute dried herbs if necessary. But do so in a ratio of:

3 parts fresh to 1 part dried

Dried herbs impart a more concentrated flavor, which is why you need less of them. For instance, if your recipe calls for three tablespoons of fresh basil, you'll be fine if you use one tablespoon of dried basil instead.

The Infamous Salt Question: What Kind Do I Use?

All life on earth began in the oceans, so it's no surprise that organisms' cellular fluids chemically resemble sea water. Saltwater in the ocean is "salty" due to many, many minerals, not just sodium chloride. We need these minerals, not coincidentally, in roughly the same proportion that they exist in… guess where?… the ocean! (You've just gotta love Mother Nature.)

So when preparing food, I always use sea salt, which can be found at any health food store. Better still is sea salt that was deposited into salt beds before the industrial revolution started spewing toxins into the world's waterways. My personal preference is Himalayan Crystal Salt, fine granules. It's mined high in the mountains from ancient sea-beds, has a beautiful pink color, and imparts more than 84 essential minerals into your diet. You can use either the Himalayan crystal variety or Celtic Sea Salt, but I would highly recommend sticking to at least one of these two. You can buy Himalayan crystal salt through KristensRaw .com/store.

Kristen Suzanne's Tip: Start Small with Strong Flavors

FLAVORS AND THEIR STRENGTH

There are certain flavors and ingredients that are particularly strong, such as garlic, ginger, onion, and salt. It's important to observe patience here, as these are flavors that can be loved or considered offensive, depending on who is eating the food. I know people who want the maximum amount of salt called for in a recipe and I know some who are highly sensitive to it. Therefore, to make the best possible Raw experience for you, I recommend starting on the "small end" especially with ingredients like garlic, ginger, strong savory herbs and seasonings, onions (any variety), citrus, and even salt. If I've given you a range in a recipe, for instance ¼–½ *teaspoon Himalayan crystal salt* then I recommend starting with the smaller amount, and then tasting it. If you don't love it, then add a little more of that ingredient and taste it again. Start small. It's worth the extra 60 seconds it might take you to do this. You might end up using less, saving it for the next recipe you make and voila, you're saving a little money.

LESSON #1: It's very hard to correct any flavors of excess, so start small and build.

LESSON #2: *Write it down.* When an ingredient offers a "range" for itself, write down the amount you liked best. If you use an "optional" ingredient, make a note about that as well.

One more thing to know about some strong flavors like the ones mentioned above... with Raw food, these flavors can intensify the finished product as each day passes. For example, the garlic in your soup, on the day you made it, might be perfect. On day two, it's still really great but a little stronger in flavor. And by day three, you might want to carry around your toothbrush or a little chewing gum!

HERE IS A TIP TO HELP CONTROL THIS

If you're making a recipe in advance, such as a dressing or soup that you won't be eating until the following day or even the day after that, then hold off on adding some of the strong seasonings until the day you eat it (think garlic and ginger). Or, if you're going to make the dressing or soup in advance, use less of the strong seasoning, knowing that it might intensify on its own by the time you eat it. This isn't a huge deal because it doesn't change that dramatically, but I mention it so you won't be surprised, especially when serving a favorite dish to others.

Kristen Suzanne's Tip: Doubling Recipes

More often than not, there are certain ingredients and flavors that you don't typically double in their entirety, if you're making a double or triple batch of a recipe. These are strong-flavored ingredients similar to those mentioned above (salt, garlic, ginger, herbs, seasoning, etc). A good rule of thumb is this: For a double batch, use 1.5 times the amount for certain ingredients. Taste it and see if you need the rest. For instance, if I'm making a "double batch" of soup, and the normal recipe calls for 1 tablespoon of Himalayan crystal salt, then I'll put in 1 ½ tablespoons to start, instead of two. Then, I'll taste it and add the remaining ½ tablespoon, if necessary.

This same principle is not necessarily followed when dividing a recipe in half. Go ahead and simply divide in half, or by whatever amount you're making. If there is a range for a particular ingredient provided, I still recommend that you use the smaller amount of an ingredient when dividing. Taste the final product and then decide whether or not to add more.

My recipes provide a variety of yields, as you'll see below. Some recipes make 2 servings and some make 4–6 servings. For those of you making food for only yourself, then simply cut the recipes making 4–6 servings in half. Or, as I always do… I make the larger serving size and then I have enough food for a couple of meals. If a recipe yields 2 servings, I usually double it for the same reason.

Kristen Suzanne's Tip: Changing Produce

"But I made it exactly like this last time! Why doesn't it taste the same?"

Here is something you need to embrace when preparing Raw vegan food. Fresh produce can vary in its composition of water, and even flavor, to some degree. There are times I've made marinara sauce and, to me, it was the perfect level of sweetness in the finished product. Then, the next time I made it, you would have thought I added a smidge of sweetener. This is due to the fact that fresh Raw produce can have a slightly different taste from time to time when you make a recipe (only ever so slightly, so don't be alarmed). *Aahhh, here is the silver lining!* This means you'll never get bored living the Raw vegan lifestyle because your recipes can change a little in flavor from time to time, even though you followed the same recipe. Embrace this natural aspect of produce and love it for everything that it is.

This is much less of an issue with cooked food. Most of the water is taken out of cooked food, so you typically get the same flavors and experience each and every time. Boring!

Kristen Suzanne's Tip: Ripeness and Storage for Your Fresh Produce

1. I never use green bell peppers because they are not "ripe." This is why so many people have a hard time digesting them (often "belching" after eating them). To truly experience the greatest health, it's important to eat fruits and vegetables at their peak ripeness. Therefore, make sure you only use red, orange, or yellow bell peppers. Store these in your refrigerator.

2. A truly ripe banana has some brown freckles or spots on the peel. This is when you're supposed to eat a banana. Store these on your countertop away from other produce, because bananas give off a gas as they ripen, which will affect the ripening process of your other produce. And, if you have a lot of bananas, split them up. This will help prevent all of your bananas from ripening at once.

3. Keep avocados on the counter until they reach ripeness (when their skin is usually brown in color and if you gently squeeze it, it "gives" just a little). At this point, you can put them in the refrigerator where they'll last up to a week longer. If you keep ripe avocados on the counter, they'll only last another couple of days. Avocados, like bananas, give off a gas as they ripen, which will affect the ripening process of your other produce. Let them ripen away from your other produce. And, if you have a lot of avocados, separate them. This will help prevent all of your avocados from ripening at once.

4. Tomatoes are best stored on your counter. Do not put them in the refrigerator or they'll get a "mealy" texture.

5. Pineapple is ripe for eating when you can gently pull a leaf out of the top of it. Therefore, test your pineapple for ripeness at the store to ensure you're buying the sweetest one possible. Just pull one of the leaves out from the top. After 3 to 4 attempts on different leaves, if you can't gently take one of them out, then move on to another pineapple.

6. Stone fruits (fruits with pits, such as peaches, plums, and nectarines), bananas and avocados all continue to ripen after being picked.

7. I have produce ripening all over my house. Sounds silly maybe, but I don't want it crowded on my kitchen countertop. I move it around and turn it over daily.

For a more complete list of produce ripening tips, check out my book, *Kristen's Raw*, available at Amazon.com.

Kristen Suzanne's Tip: Proper Dehydration Techniques

Dehydrating your Raw vegan food at a low temperature is a technique that warms and dries the food while preserving its nutritional integrity. When using a dehydrator, it is recommended that you begin the dehydrating process at a temperature of 130–140 degrees F for about an hour. Then, lower the temperature to 105 degrees F for the remaining time of dehydration. Using a high temperature such as 140 degrees F, *in the initial stages of dehydration*, does not destroy the nutritional value of the food. During this initial phase, the food does the most "sweating" (releasing moisture), which cools the food. Therefore, while the temperature of the air circulating *around* the food is about 140 degrees F, the food itself is much cooler. These directions apply only when using an Excalibur Dehydrator because of their Horizontal-Airflow Drying System. Furthermore, I am happy to only recommend Excalibur dehydrators because of their first-class products and customer service. For details, visit the *Raw Kitchen Essential Tools* section of my website at KristensRaw.com/store.

MY YIELD AND SERVING AMOUNTS NOTED IN THE RECIPES

Each recipe in this book shows an approximate amount that the recipe yields (the quantity it makes). I find that "one serving" to me might be considered two servings to someone else, or vice versa. Therefore, I tried to use an "average" when listing the serving amount. Don't let that stop you from eating a two-serving dish in one sitting, if it seems like the right amount for you. It simply depends on how hungry you are.

WHAT IS THE DIFFERENCE BETWEEN CHOPPED, DICED, AND MINCED?

Chop

Chopping gives relatively uniform cuts, but doesn't need to be perfectly neat or even. You'll often be asked to chop something before putting it into a blender or food processor, which is why it doesn't have to be uniform size since it'll be getting blended or pureed.

Dice

This produces a nice cube shape, and can be different sizes, depending on which you prefer. This is great for vegetables.

Mince

This produces an even, very fine cut, typically used for fresh herbs, onions, garlic and ginger.

Julienne

This is a fancy term for long, rectangular cuts.

WHAT EQUIPMENT DO I NEED FOR MY NEW RAW FOOD KITCHEN?

I go into much more detail regarding the perfect setup for your Raw vegan kitchen in my book, *Kristen's Raw*, which is a must read for anybody who wants to learn the easy ways to succeed with living the Raw vegan lifestyle. Here are the main pieces of equipment you'll want to get you going:

1. An excellent chef's knife (6–8 inches in length—non-serrated). Of everything you do with Raw food, you'll be chopping and cutting the most, so invest in a great knife. This truly makes doing all the chopping really fun!

2. Blender

3. Food Processor (get a 7 or 10-cup or more)

4. Juicer

5. Spiralizer or Turning Slicer

6. Dehydrator—Excalibur® is the best company by far and is available at KristensRaw.com

7. Salad spinner

8. Other knives (paring, serrated)

For links to online retailers that sell my favorite kitchen tools and foods, visit KristensRaw.com/store.

SOAKING AND DEHYDRATING NUTS AND SEEDS

This is an important topic. When using nuts and seeds in Raw vegan foods, you'll find that recipes sometimes call for them to be "soaked" or "soaked and dehydrated." Here is the low-down on the importance and the difference between the two.

Why Should You Soak Your Nuts and Seeds?

Most nuts and seeds come packed by Mother Nature with enzyme inhibitors, rendering them harder to digest. These inhibitors essentially shut down the nuts' and seeds' metabolic activity, rendering them dormant—for as long as they need to be—until they detect a moisture-rich environment that's suitable for germination (e.g., rain). By soaking your nuts and seeds, you trick the nuts into "waking up," shutting off the inhibitors so that the enzymes can become active. This greatly enhances the nuts' digestibility for you and is highly recommended if you want to experience Raw vegan food in the healthiest way possible.

Even though you'll want to soak the nuts to activate their enzymes, before using them, you'll need to re-dry them and grind them down anywhere from coarse to fine (into a powder almost like flour), depending on the recipe. To dry them, you'll need a dehydrator. (If you don't own a dehydrator yet, then, if a recipe calls for "soaked and dehydrated," just skip the soaking part; you can use the nuts or seeds in the dry form that you bought them).

Drying your nuts (but not yet grinding them) is a great thing to do before storing them in the freezer or refrigerator (preferably in glass mason jars). They will last a long time and you'll always have them on hand, ready to use.

In my recipes, I use nuts and seeds that are "soaked and dehydrated" (that is, dry) unless otherwise stated in the directions as needing to be soaked (wet).

Some nuts and seeds don't have to follow the enzyme inhibitor rule; therefore, they don't need to be soaked. These are:

- Macadamia nuts
- Brazil nuts
- Pine nuts
- Hemp seeds
- Most cashews

An additional note... there are times when the recipe will call for soaking, even though it's for a type of nut or seed without enzyme inhibitors, such as Brazil nuts. The logic behind this is to help *soften* the nuts so they blend into a smoother texture, especially if you don't have a high-powered blender. This is helpful when making nut milks, soups and sauces.

Instructions for "Soaking" and "Soaking and Dehydrating" Nuts

"SOAKING"

The general rule to follow: Any nuts or seeds that require soaking can be soaked overnight (6–10 hours). Put the required amount of nuts or seeds into a bowl and add enough water to cover by about an inch or so. Set them on your counter overnight. The following morning, or 6–10 hours after you soaked them, drain and rinse them. They are now ready to eat or use in a recipe. At this point, they need to be refrigerated in an airtight container (preferably a glass mason jar) and they'll have a shelf life of about 3 days maximum. Only soak the amount you're going to need or eat, unless you plan on dehydrating them right away.

A note about flax seeds and chia seeds... these don't need to be soaked if your recipe calls for grinding them into a powder. Some recipes will call to soak the seeds in their "whole-seed" form, before making crackers and bread, because they create a very gelatinous and binding texture when soaked. You can soak flax or chia seeds in a ratio of one-part seeds to two-parts water, and they can be soaked for as short as 1 hour and up to 12 hours. At this point, they are ready to use (don't drain them). Personally, when I use flax seeds, I usually grind them and don't soak them. It's hard for your body to digest "whole" flax seeds, even if they are soaked. It's much easier for your body to assimilate the nutrients when they're ground to a flax meal.

"SOAKING AND DEHYDRATING"

Follow the same directions for soaking. Then, after draining and rinsing the nuts, spread them out on a mesh dehydrator sheet and dehydrate them at 140 degrees F for one hour. Lower the temperature to 105 degrees F and dehydrate them until they're completely dry, which can take up to 24 hours.

Please note, all nuts and seeds called for in my recipes will always be "Raw and Organic" and "Soaked and Dehydrated" unless the recipe calls for soaking.

ALMOND PULP

Some of my recipes call for "almond pulp," which is really easy to make. After making your fresh almond milk (see Nut/Seed Milk recipe, Appendix A) and straining it through a "nut milk bag," (available at NaturalZing.com or you can use a paint strainer bag from the hardware store—much cheaper), you will find a nice, soft pulp inside the bag. Turn the bag inside out and flatten the pulp out onto a ParaFlexx dehydrator sheet with a spatula or your hand. Dehydrate the pulp at 140 degrees F for one hour, then lower the temperature to 105 degrees F and continue dehydrating until the almond pulp is dry (up to 24 hours). Break the pulp into chunks and store in the freezer until you're ready to use it. Before using the almond pulp, grind it into a flour in your blender or food processor.

SOY LECITHIN

Some recipes (desserts, in particular) will call for soy lecithin, which is extracted from soybean oil. This optional ingredient is not Raw. If you use soy lecithin, I highly recommend using a brand that is "non-GMO," meaning it was processed without any genetically modified ingredients (a great brand is Health Alliance®). Soy lecithin helps your dessert (cheesecake, for example) maintain a firmer texture.

There is another lecithin option on the market, Sunflower Lecithin. This is used as an emulsifier in recipes. Soy lecithin is a common "go-to" source, but not everyone wants a soy product. That's all changed now that sunflower lecithin is available. You can find a link to purchase it at KristensRaw.com/store.

ICE CREAM FLAVORINGS

When making Raw vegan ice cream, it's better to use alcohol-free extracts so they freeze better.

SWEETENERS

The following is a list of sweeteners that you might see used in my recipes. It's important to know that the healthiest sweeteners are fresh whole fruits, including fresh dates. That said, dates sometimes compromise texture in recipes. As a chef, I look for great texture, and as a health food advocate, I lean towards fresh dates. But as a consultant helping people embrace a Raw vegan lifestyle, I'm also supportive of helping them transition, which sometimes means using raw agave nectar, or some other easy-to-use sweetener that might not have the healthiest ranking in the Raw food world, but is still much healthier than most sweeteners used in the Standard American Diet.

Most of my recipes can use pitted dates in place of raw agave nectar. There is some debate among Raw food enthusiasts as to whether agave nectar is Raw. The company I primarily use (Madhava®) claims to be Raw and says they do not heat their Raw agave nectar above 118 degrees F. If however, you still want to eat the healthiest of sweeteners, then bypass the raw agave nectar and use pitted dates. In most recipes, you can simply substitute 1–2 pitted dates for 1 tablespoon of raw agave nectar. Dates will not give you a super creamy texture, but the texture can be improved by making a "date paste" (pureeing pitted and soaked dates—with their soak water, plus some additional water, if necessary—in a food processor fitted with the "S" blade). This, of course, takes a little extra time.

If using raw agave nectar is easier and faster for you, then go ahead and use it; just be sure to buy the raw version that says they don't heat the agave above 118 degrees F. And, again, if you're looking to go as far as you can on the spectrum of health, then I recommend using pitted dates. Many of my recipes use raw agave nectar because that is most convenient for people.

Raw Agave Nectar

There are a variety of agave nectars on the market, but again, not all of them are Raw. Make sure it is labeled "Raw" on the bottle *as well as claiming that it isn't processed above 118 degrees F.* Just because the label says "Raw" does not necessarily mean it is so... do a double check and make sure it also claims "not to be heated above 118 degrees F." Agave nectar is noteworthy for having a low glycemic index.

Dates

Dates are probably the healthiest of sweeteners, because they're a fresh whole food (I'm a big fan of Medjool dates). Fresh organic dates are filled with nutrition, including calcium and magnesium. I like to call dates, "Nature's Candy."

Feel free to use dates instead of agave or honey in raw vegan recipes. If a recipe calls for ½ cup of raw agave, then you can substitute with approximately ½ cup of pitted dates (or more).

You can also make a recipe of Date Paste to replace raw agave (or to use in combination with it). It's not always as sweet as agave, so you might want to adjust the amount according to your taste by using a bit more Date Paste (see recipe, Appendix A).

Honey

Most honey is technically raw, but it is not vegan by most definitions of "vegan" because it is produced by animals, who therefore are at risk of being mistreated. While honey does not have the health risks associated with animal byproducts such as eggs or dairy, it can spike the body's natural sugar levels. Agave nectar has a lower, healthier glycemic index and can replace any recipe you find that calls for honey, in a 1 to 1 ratio.

Maple Syrup

Maple syrup is made from boiled sap of the maple tree. It is not considered raw, but some people still use it as a sweetener in certain dishes.

Rapadura®

This is a dried sugarcane juice, and it's not raw. It is, however, an unrefined and unbleached organic whole-cane sugar. It imparts a nice deep sweetness to your recipes, even if you only use a little. Feel free to omit it if you'd like to adhere to a strictly Raw program.

Stevia

This is from the leaf of the stevia plant. It has a sweet taste and doesn't elevate blood sugar levels. It's very sweet, so you'll want to use much less stevia than you would any other sweetener. My mom actually grows her own stevia. It's a great addition in fresh smoothies, for example, to add some sweetness without the calories. When possible, the best way to have stevia is grow it yourself.

Yacon Syrup

This sweetener has a low glycemic index, making it very attractive to some people. It has a molasses-type flavor that is very enjoyable. You can replace raw agave with this sweetener, but keep in mind that it's not as sweet in flavor as raw agave nectar. The brand I usually buy is Navitas Naturals, which is available at NavitasNaturals.com. For more information, see Appendix B, Resources.

SUN-DRIED TOMATOES

By far, the best sun-dried tomatoes are those you make yourself with a dehydrator. If you don't have a dehydrator, make sure you buy the "dry" sun-dried tomatoes, usually found in the bulk section of your health food market. Don't buy the kind that are packed in a jar of oil.

Also... don't buy sun-dried tomatoes if they're really dark (almost black) because these just don't taste as good. Again, I recommend making them yourself if you truly want the freshest flavor possible. It's really fun to do!

EATING WITH YOUR EYES

Most of us, if not all, naturally eat with our eyes before taking a bite of food. So, do yourself a favor and make your eating experience the best ever with the help of a simple, gorgeous presentation. Think of it this way, with real estate, it's always *location, location, location*, right? Well, with food, it's always *presentation, presentation, presentation*.

Luckily, Raw food does this on its own with all of its naturally vibrant and bright colors. But I take it even one step farther—I use my best dishes when I eat. I use my beautiful wine glasses for my smoothies and juices. I use my fancy goblets for many of my desserts. Why? Because I'm worth it. And, so are you! Don't save your good china just for company. Believe me, you'll notice the difference. Eating well is an attitude, and when you take care of yourself, your body will respond in kind.

ONLINE RESOURCES FOR GREAT PRODUCTS

For a complete and detailed list of my favorite kitchen tools, products, and various foods (all available online), please visit: KristensRaw.com/store.

BOOK & DVD RECOMMENDATIONS

I highly recommend reading the following life-changing books and DVDs.

- *Diet for a New America,* by John Robbins
- *The Food Revolution,* by John Robbins
- *The China Study,* by T. Colin Campbell
- *Skinny Bitch,* by Rory Freedman
- *Food, Inc.* (DVD)
- *Food Matters* (DVD)
- *The Future of Food* (DVD)
- *Earthlings* (DVD)

MEASUREMENT CONVERSIONS

1 tablespoon = 3 teaspoons

1 ounce = 2 tablespoons

¼ cup = 4 tablespoons

⅓ cup = 5 ⅓ tablespoons

1 cup = 8 ounces

= 16 tablespoons

= ½ pint

½ quart = 1 pint

= 2 cups

1 gallon = 4 quarts

= 8 pints

= 16 cups

= 128 ounces

Nourishing Rejuvelac

Yield 1 gallon

Rejuvelac is a cheesy-tasting liquid that is rich in enzymes and healthy flora to support a healthy intestine and digestion. Get comfortable making this super easy recipe because its use goes beyond just drinking it between meals.

Some people are concerned about the wheat aspect to wheat berries being used in most Rejuvelac recipes. While many people easily tolerate Rejuvelac made with wheat berries in spite of having wheat intolerance issues, there are other ingredients you can use to make Rejuvelac wheat-free. Some options are buckwheat, rice, quinoa, and more.

1 cup soft wheat berries, rye berries, or a mixture

water

Place the wheat berries in a half-gallon jar and fill the jar with water. Screw the lid on the jar and soak the wheat berries overnight (10–12 hours) on your counter. The next morning, drain and rinse them. Sprout the wheat berries for 2 days, draining and rinsing 1–2 times a day.

Then, fill the jar with purified water and screw on the lid, or cover with cheesecloth secured with a rubber band. Allow to ferment for 24–36 hours, or until the desired tartness is achieved. It should have a cheesy, almost tart/lemony flavor and scent.

Strain your rejuvelac into another glass jar and store in the refrigerator for up to 5–7 days. For a second batch using the same sprouted wheat berries, fill the same jar of already sprouted berries with water again, and allow to ferment for 24 hours. Strain off the rejuvelac as you did the time before this. You can do this process yet again, noting that each time the rejuvelac gets a little weaker in flavor.

Enjoy ¼–1 cup of Nourishing Rejuvelac first thing in the morning and/or between meals. It's best to start with a small amount and work your way up as your body adjusts.

Suggestion:

- For extra nutrition and incredible flavor, Nourishing Rejuvelac can be used in various recipes such as raw vegan cheeses, desserts, smoothies, soups, dressings and more. Simply use it in place of the water required by the recipe.

Date Paste

It's great to keep this on hand in the refrigerator so you have it available and ready to use. Date Paste is easy to make and should take you less than 10 minutes to prepare once your dates are soaked. Store it in an airtight container in the refrigerator (a glass mason jar is perfect).

> **15 medjool dates, pitted, soaked 15 minutes (reserve soak water)**
>
> **¼–½ cup reserved "soak water"**

Using a food processor, fitted with the "S" blade, puree the ingredients until you have a smooth paste.

Crème Fraiche

Yield approximately 2 cups

1 cup raw cashews

¼–½ cup Nourishing Rejuvelac (see recipe, Appendix A)

1–2 tablespoons raw agave nectar

Place the cashews in a bowl and cover with enough water by about an inch. Let them soak for 1 hour. Drain off the water and give them a quick rinse.

Blend the ingredients until smooth. Store in an airtight glass mason jar for up to 5 days. This freezes well, so feel free to make a double batch for future use.

Nut/Seed Milk (regular)

The creamiest nut/seed milk traditionally comes from hemp seeds, cashews, pine nuts, Brazil nuts or macadamia nuts, although I'm also a huge fan of milks made from walnuts, pecans, hazelnuts, almonds, sesame seeds, sunflower seeds, and pumpkin seeds.

This recipe does not include a sweetener, but when I'm in the mood for a little sweetness, I add a couple of pitted dates or a squirt of raw agave nectar. Yum!

> 1 ½ cups raw nuts or seeds
>
> 3 ¼ cups water
>
> pinch Himalayan crystal salt, optional

Place the nuts in a bowl and cover with enough water by about an inch. Let them soak for 6-8 hours (unless you're using cashews, pine nuts, Brazil nuts, or macadamia nuts, in which case you only have to soak them about an hour. Hemp seeds do not need soaking because they're very soft and easy to blend, but adjust the amount of water used in the recipe, as needed). Drain off the water and give them a quick rinse.

Blend the ingredients until smooth and deliciously creamy. For an even *extra creamy* texture, strain your nut/seed milk through a nut milk bag.

Sweet Nut/Seed Cream (thick)

Yield 2–3 cups

1 cup raw nuts or seeds

1–1 ½ cups water, more if needed

2–3 tablespoons raw agave nectar or 3–4 dates, pitted

½ teaspoon vanilla extract, optional

Place the nuts in a bowl and cover with enough water by about an inch. Let them soak for 6–8 hours (unless you're using cashews, pine nuts, Brazil nuts, or macadamia nuts, in which case you only have to soak them about an hour. Hemp seeds do not need soaking because they're very soft and easy to blend, but adjust the amount of water used in the recipe, as needed). Drain off the water and give them a quick rinse.

Blend all of the ingredients until smooth.

Raw Mustard

2 teaspoons yellow mustard seeds, soaked 1–2 hours, then drained

½ cup extra virgin olive oil or hemp oil

1 tablespoon dry mustard powder

1 tablespoon apple cider vinegar

1 tablespoon fresh lemon juice or lime juice

¼ cup raw agave nectar

½ teaspoon Himalayan crystal salt

¼ teaspoon turmeric

Blend all of the ingredients together until smooth. It might be very thick, so if you want, add some water or oil to help thin it out. Adding more oil will help reduce the "heat" if it's too spicy for your taste.

Variation:

- "Honey" Mustard Version: Add more raw agave nectar (until you reach the desired sweetness)

My Basic Raw Mayonnaise

Yield about 2 ½ cups

People tell me all the time how much they like this recipe.

- 1 cup raw cashews
- ½ teaspoon paprika
- 2 cloves garlic
- 1 teaspoon onion powder
- 3 tablespoons fresh lemon juice
- ¼ cup extra virgin olive oil or hemp oil
- 2 tablespoons parsley, chopped
- 2 tablespoons water, if needed

Place the cashews in a bowl and cover with enough water by about an inch. Let them soak for 1 hour. Drain off the water and give them a quick rinse.

Blend all of the ingredients, except the parsley, until creamy. Pulse in the parsley. My Basic Raw Mayonnaise will stay fresh for up to one week in the refrigerator.

Appendix B

• • • • • • • • • •

Resources

The resources listed in this appendix are mostly raw, but you will also see a few items that are not raw.

BANANAS (FROZEN)

To make frozen bananas, simply peel (ripe) bananas, place them in a baggie or container, and put them in the freezer. I like to use my FoodSaver®, because it keeps the bananas from getting ice crystals on them. Having frozen bananas in your freezer at all times is a smart move. They are fantastic in smoothies, and they make a deliciously fun raw ice cream (just throw them in the food processor and puree them into a soft serve, raw vegan ice cream).

BREAD (SPROUTED)

You can buy this at the health food store. A couple of my favorite brands are *Good for Life* and *Manna Organics*.

CACAO LIQUOR (RAW)

This is the result of whole cacao beans that have been peeled and cold-pressed, which forms a paste. I use this to make a number of raw chocolate recipes. It comes in a block form and I melt it into a thick liquid using my dehydrator (or you can use a double boiler). It's bitter so I add sweetener. This is available from NavitasNaturals.com

CACAO NIBS (RAW)

These are partially ground cacao beans. They can be used in a variety of ways from toppings to raw vegan ice cream or yogurt. They add texture to shakes and smoothies, and you can make raw chocolates with them. They are available from NavitasNaturals .com and other sources online.

CAROB (RAW)

A lot of the carob you find in the store is toasted. I like to use raw carob, which has a wonderful flavor (caramel-like) and can be used in many recipes such as smoothies, nut milks, desserts, and more. There is a link for raw carob at KristensRaw.com/store.

CHIA SEEDS

These are called the "Dieter's Dream Food." Chia seeds are praised for many things including their fantastic nutrient profile, which proudly boasts iron, boron, essential fatty acids, fiber, and more. Add to that the claims that they may improve heart health, reduce blood pressure, stabilize blood sugar, help people lose weight from giving them extra stamina, energy, and curbing hunger, and you might become a fan of these little guys, too. They're superstars in my book. You can find a link for them at KristensRaw.com/store.

CHOCOLATE (CACAO) POWDER (RAW)

This is formed after the whole cacao beans have been peeled and cold-pressed. Then, the cacao oil is extracted and a powder remains. I use this in many recipes from making raw chocolate desserts to smoothies to soups to dressings and more. This is available from NavitasNaturals.com and other sources online.

COCONUT AMINOS

This is a seasoning sauce that can be used in place of tamari and namo shoyu. Available from the company, Coconut Secret, it's raw, enzymatically alive, organic, gluten-free, and soy-free. For more details, check out CoconutSecret.com. It's also available at some Whole Foods Markets.

COCONUT BUTTER OR *COCONUT SPREAD*

Coconut butter is not to be confused with plain coconut oil. Coconut butter is actually the coconut oil and coconut meat together in one jar. This can be eaten by the spoonful and it can also be used in desserts, smoothies, spreads, and more. There are two companies that I buy this from: WildernessFamilyNaturals.com offers a product they call "Coconut Spread" while Artisana calls theirs coconut butter. You can find the Artisana Coconut Butter at many health food stores including Whole Foods Market.

To make coconut butter easier (i.e., softer) to use, consider warming it in a dehydrator (at a low temperature).

DIAYA™ CHEESE

This is an amazing vegan cheese (not raw) that is taking the vegan world by storm. If you know of someone who misses artery-clogging, animal based cheese, then turn them on to this. It's soy-free, dairy-free, gluten-free, corn-free, and preservative-free. You can read more details at DaiyaFoods.com. I buy it from Whole Foods Market.

GOLDENBERRIES

These are also known as Incan Berries or Cape Gooseberries. They are basically a little dried fruit similar in shape to a raisin, and golden in color. The first time I tried these, I immediately thought, *"Move over crappy sour patch kids, it's time for something way more delish and oh-so-healthy at the same time!"* Goldenberries will throw a party in your mouth. These are available at NavitasNaturals .com

GOJI BERRIES

These little ruby colored jewels (also known as wolfberries) are a mega popular superfood because of their amazing nutrient content. They have 18 amino acids, including the 8 essential amino acids. Plus, their antioxidants are through the roof! The taste is a cross between a dried cherry and dried cranberry. I enjoy them plain and used in various recipes. My favorite source for them is Navitas Naturals (they're also available at various health food stores), and there is a link for them at KristensRaw.com/store.

GREEN POWDER(S)

Green powders are chock-full of powerful raw and alkalizing nutrition. My favorites are *Health Force Nutritionals' Vitamineral Green* and *Amazing Grass' Wheat Grass Powder*. Health Force Nutritionals also makes a green powder for pets called *Green Mush*. You will find links to these products at KristensRaw.com/store.

HEMP FOODS

Hemp is commonly referred to as a "superfood" because of its amazing nutritional value. Its amino acid profile dominates with the 8 essential amino acids (10 if you're elderly or a baby), making it a vegetarian source of "complete" protein. Manitoba Harvest is my favorite source for hemp products. I use their hemp seeds, hemp butter, hemp protein powder and hemp oil to make many delicious raw vegan recipes.

HERBAMERE™

This is an alternative to plain salt. It is a blend of sea salt and 14 organic herbs. It's a nice change of pace from plain salt. This is available on Amazon.com, other websites, and in some health food stores.

LUCUMA POWDER

Lucuma is a fun ingredient that is popular with Raw fooders. NavitasNaturals.com offers lucuma as a whole food powder, which adds a lovely sweetness to recipes with a flavor that has been described as a cross between sweet potato and maple. I love using lucuma powder in various raw recipes for smoothies, ice cream, cheesecake, nut milk, cookies, brownies, and more. There are other online sources for lucuma powder as well.

MACA POWDER

Maca is a plant that is used as a root and medicinal herb. Many people claim it gives them tons of energy and increased stamina for exercise, long workdays, and even libido! Personally, I'm not a huge fan of maca's flavor (to me, it smells like feet and tastes accordingly—haha), but this is one of the most popular superfoods among Raw vegans (so many people love it!), and for good reason with its reputed benefits. (Did I mention libido?) There is a link for maca powder at KristensRaw.com/store.

MESQUITE POWDER

This comes in a powder form that offers nutrition with a smoky, malt-like, and caramel flavor. This is available from NavitasNaturals .com and other online sources.

MISO

My all-time favorite source of organic miso is South River Miso. It's the ONLY brand I use. They have so many amazing flavors (including soy-free varieties). Check them out at SouthRiver-Miso.com. Two of my favorite flavors are *Dandelion Leek* and *Garlic Red Pepper*. You can use other brands of light or dark miso in place of the fancier flavors I've used in these recipes, but South River Miso is amazing so I highly recommend it.

MULBERRIES

These are lightly sweet with a wonderful texture that makes it hard to stop eating them. I consider these delights a superfood because of their nutrient content, including a decent source of protein. They are available from NavitasNaturals.com.

NON-DAIRY (PLANT-BASED) MILK

There are plenty of plant-based milks available for purchase in various grocery stores. They are not raw, but they are vegan and many are available as organic, which I highly recommend. Here are some options: almond, hemp, rice, soy, hazelnut, oat, and coconut. Plus, there are different flavors within those varieties such as plain, vanilla, and chocolate.

NUT / SEED BUTTERS (RAW)

Raw nut butters can be bought at most health food stores or you can easily make your own (simply grind nuts with a dash of Himalayan crystal salt in a food processor, fitted with the "S" blade, until you get a nut or seed butter. You might choose to add a little olive oil to help facilitate the processing. This could take 3–8 minutes).

There are different varieties available such as hemp seed butter, almond butter, hazelnut butter, pecan butter, sunflower seed butter, pumpkin seed butter, cashew butter, walnut butter, macadamia nut butter, and more. Some excellent brands are *Living Tree Community, Rejuvenative Brands, Wilderness Poets (online)*, and *Artisana*. I usually buy them from Whole Foods Market.

OLIVES (RAW)

I truly love *Essential Living Foods'* Black Bojita Olives. They are juicy, fresh, and delicious. It's hard to stop at eating only one! They are available at Whole Foods Market and online at EssentialLivingFoods.com. I also use *Living Tree Community's* Sun-Dried Olives in some recipes. They're different in taste and texture than the Black Bojita Olives.

OLIVE OIL (RAW)

I enjoy two truly raw olive oils: *Living Tree Community* (LivingTreeCommunity.com, also available at some Whole Foods Markets) and *Wilderness Family Naturals* (available online at WildernessFamilyNaturals.com).

ORANGE PEEL POWDER

This is a powder, which is the dried, finely ground orange peel (it's where you'll find many of the orange's nutrients, too). This is available from MountainRoseHerbs.com (They also have lemon peel powder.)

PROTEIN POWDER

I use various raw vegan protein powders to get extra protein in my life. My favorites are hemp and sprouted raw brown rice protein powders.

In general, when I'm drinking the sprouted raw brown rice protein powder (by just mixing it with water), I like the chocolate and natural flavors from *Sun Warrior* or the plain flavor of *Sprout Living's EPIC Protein*. Hemp foods, *Sun Warrior* protein powder and *Sprout Living* protein powder are available at KristensRaw.com/store.

RAPADURA

This is a dried sugarcane juice, and it is not Raw. It is, however, an unrefined and unbleached organic whole-cane sugar. I buy mine at Whole Foods Market.

RIGHTEOUSLY RAW CACAO BARS (EARTH SOURCE ORGANICS)

Even though this is not an ingredient in which you'd use to make a recipe, I had to mention it here (it's an actual product for organic, raw, vegan chocolate bars). In my opinion, this is the best raw chocolate bar on the market. My favorite flavor is the Caramel Cacao but they also sell Goji, Maca, and Acai. Sometimes I just don't have time to make my own raw chocolate and sometimes I'm just plain lazy. In both cases, I run to Whole Foods Market for these (you can also buy them online direct from the company: earthsourceorganics.com). If your Whole Foods doesn't stock these... tell them to do it! Check out my blog post where I talked about my first encounter with these divine treats.

http://kristensraw.blogspot.com/2010/review-earth-source-organics.html

ROLLED OATS

I use traditional organic oats from SunOrganic.com or raw oats available at NaturalZing.com.

SAUERKRAUT (RAW, UNPASTEURIZED)

You can buy sauerkraut from the health food store or make it yourself (my favorite way). If you choose to buy it from the store, be sure to get a brand that is organic, raw, and unpasteurized. Two brands that I like are *Gold Mine Natural Foods* and *Rejuvenative Foods* (they're both great, but my overall preference is Gold Mine Natural Foods).

However, making your own is the best. It's incredibly easy and fun. For directions on making your own sauerkraut, please see my blog posts and video here:

http://kristensraw.blogspot.com/2009/07/how-to-make-sauerkraut-video-raw.html

SESAME OIL (RAW)

You can get this from RejuvenativeFoods.com.

STEVIA

Stevia is an all-natural sweetener from the stevia plant. It has a sweet taste and doesn't elevate blood sugar levels. It is very sweet, so you will want to use much less stevia than you would any other sweetener. I buy mine from Navitas Naturals (available at NavitasNaturals.com)

SUN-DRIED OLIVES

I buy the brand *Living Tree Community* at Whole Foods Market or online at LivingTreeCommunity.com.

SUNFLOWER LECITHIN

This is popular for its choline content, and it's also used as an emulsifier in recipes. Soy lecithin is a common "go-to" source for this purpose, but not everyone wants a soy product. That is all changed now that sunflower lecithin is available. I like adding it to raw soups, smoothies, desserts, and more. You can find a link for it at KristensRaw.com/store.

TEECCINO®

This is an alkaline herbal "coffee" (it's not really coffee) that my family loves since giving up regular coffee. It is available at many health food stores like Whole Foods Market. It's also available online (Amazon.com). For details about the awesomeness of this product, check out Teeccino.com.

VEGGIE BURGER

I LOVE Organic *Sunshine Burgers* veggie burgers, which I buy in the freezer department of Whole Foods Market. Check out their website at SunshineBurger.com.

WAKAME FLAKES

The wakame flakes that I use are from Navitas Naturals. Here is what they have to say about this particular product on their website at NavitasNaturals.com:

"One of the most hearty vegetables of the sea, wakame is in fact an algae that is amongst the oldest living species on Earth. This sea green has been used extensively in traditional Japanese, Chinese, and Korean cuisine as an important health food and key component of Eastern medicine for centuries. Wakame is a balanced combination of essential organic minerals including iron, calcium, and magnesium, alongside valuable trace minerals as well. Additionally, wakame is well known for its detoxifying antioxidants, Omega 3 fatty acids (in the form of Eicospentaenoic acid), and body-building vegetable proteins. Wakame also provides many vitamins like vitamin C and much of the B spectrum, and serves as an excellent source of both soluble and insoluble fiber."

Impressive, huh?

WHEAT GRASS POWDER

I use Amazing Grass' Wheat Grass Powder available at KristensRaw.com/store.

YACON SYRUP, POWDER, AND SLICES

This is an alternative sweetener offering a low glycemic index so it's commonly viewed as diabetic friendly. According to Navitas-Naturals.com (the brand I prefer for yacon products), *"... yacon tastes sweet, the sugar of inulin is not digestible and simply passes through the body. Therefore, yacon only contains about half the calories of an average sugar source. Secondly, FOS (promotes the production of healthy probiotics within the body, which can contribute to better digestion and colon health."*

As a reader of this book, you are entitled to a 10% discount off Excalibur dehydrators and products:

CPSIA information can be obtained at www.ICGtesting.com
Printed in the USA
BVOW08s1011150415

396271BV00022B/375/P